YOUR PERSONAL
HOROSCOPE
2018

LIBRA

Your Personal Horoscope 2018

Libra
24th September–23rd October

igloobooks

igloobooks

Published in 2017
by Igloo Books Ltd
Cottage Farm
Sywell
NN6 0BJ
www.igloobooks.com

Produced for Igloo Books by Foulsham Publishing Ltd, The Old Barrel Store,
Drayman's Lane, Marlow, Bucks SL7 2FF, England

FIR003 0717
2 4 6 8 10 9 7 5 3 1
ISBN: 978-1-78670-882-3

This is an abridged version of material originally published
in Old Moore's Horoscope and Astral Diary.

Cover design by Charles Wood-Penn
Edited by Jasmin Peppiatt

Printed and manufactured in China

CONTENTS

CONTENTS

INTRODUCTION

Your Personal Horoscopes have been specifically created to allow you to get the most from astrological patterns and the way they have a bearing on not only your zodiac sign, but nuances within it. Using the diary section of the book you can read about the influences and possibilities of each and every day of the year. It will be possible for you to see when you are likely to be cheerful and happy or those times when your nature is in retreat and you will be more circumspect. The diary will help to give you a feel for the specific 'cycles' of astrology and the way they can subtly change your day-to-day life. For example, when you see the sign ☿, this means that the planet Mercury is retrograde at that time. Retrograde means it appears to be running backwards through the zodiac. Such a happening has a significant effect on communication skills, but this is only one small aspect of how the Personal Horoscope can help you.

With Your Personal Horoscope the story doesn't end with the diary pages. It includes simple ways for you to work out the zodiac sign the Moon occupied at the time of your birth, and what this means for your personality. In addition, if you know the time of day you were born, it is possible to discover your Ascendant, yet another important guide to your personal make-up and potential.

Many readers are interested in relationships and in knowing how well they get on with people of other astrological signs. You might also be interested in the way you appear to very different sorts of individuals. If you are such a person, the section on Venus will be of particular interest. Despite the rapidly changing position of this planet, you can work out your Venus sign, and learn what bearing it will have on your life.

Using Your Personal Horoscope you can travel on one of the most fascinating and rewarding journeys that anyone can take – the journey to a better realisation of self.

THE ESSENCE OF LIBRA

Exploring the Personality of Libra the Scales

(24TH SEPTEMBER – 23RD OCTOBER)

What's in a sign?

At heart you may be the least complicated of all the zodiac sign types, though your ruling element is Air, and that is always going to supply some surprises. Diplomatic, kind and affectionate, your nature blows like a refreshing breeze through the lives of almost anyone you meet. It isn't like you to be gloomy for very long at a time, and you know how to influence the world around you.

It's true that you don't like dirt, or too much disorganisation, and you tend to be very artistic by inclination. You get your own way in life, not by dint of making yourself unpopular in any way but rather with the sort of gentle persuasion to which almost everyone you know falls victim at one time or another. Being considerate of others is more or less second nature to you, though you may not be quite as self-sacrificing as sometimes appears to be the case. You definitely know what you want from life and are not above using a little subterfuge when it comes to getting it.

You are capable and resourceful, but just a little timid on occasions. All the same, when dealing with subject matter that you know and relish, few can better you out there in the practical world. You know how to order your life and can be just as successful in a career sense as you tend to be in your home life. There are times when personal attractions can be something of a stumbling block because you love readily and are very influenced by the kindness and compliments of those around you.

Librans do need to plan ahead, but don't worry about this fact too much because you are also extremely good at thinking on your feet. Getting others to do your bidding is a piece of cake because you are not tardy when it comes to showing your affections. Nevertheless you need to be careful not to allow yourself to fall into unreliable company, or to get involved in schemes that seem too good to be true – some of them are. But for most of the time you present a happy picture to the world and get along just fine, with your ready smile and adaptable personality. You leave almost any situation happier and more contented than it was when you arrived.

Libra resources

When it comes to getting on in life you have as much ammunition in your armoury as most zodiac signs and a great deal more than some. For starters you are adaptable and very resourceful. When you have to take a leap in logic there is nothing preventing you from doing so, and the strong intuition of which your zodiac sign is capable can prove to be very useful at times.

One of your strongest points is the way you manage to make others love you. Although you might consider yourself to be distinctly 'ordinary', that's not the way the world at large perceives you. Most Librans have the ability to etch themselves onto the minds of practically everyone they come across. Why? It's simple. You listen to what people have to say and appear to be deeply interested. On most occasions you are, but even if the tale is a tedious one you give the impression of being rooted to the spot with a determination to hear the story right through. When it comes to responding you are extremely diplomatic and always manage to steer a sensible course between any two or more opposing factions.

Having said that you don't like dirt or untidy places, this is another fact that you can turn to your advantage, because you can always find someone who will help you out. So charming can Libra be that those who do all they can to make you more comfortable regularly end up feeling that you have done them a favour.

It is the sheer magic of the understated Libran that does the trick every time. Even on those rare occasions when you go out with all guns blazing to get what you want from life, you are very unlikely to make enemies on the way. Of course you do have to be careful on occasions, like everyone, but you can certainly push issues further than most. Why? Mainly because people don't realise that you are doing so.

You could easily sell any commodity – though it might be necessary to believe in it yourself first. Since you can always see the good points in anything and tend to be generally optimistic, that should not be too problematical either.

Beneath the surface

In many respects Libra could be the least complicated sign of the zodiac so it might be assumed that 'what you see is what you get'. Life is rarely quite that simple, though you are one of the most straightforward people when it comes to inner struggle. The fact is that most Librans simply don't have a great deal. Between subconscious motivation and in-your-face action there is a seamless process. Librans do need to be loved and this fact can be quite a strong motivation in itself towards any particular course of action. However, even this desire for affection isn't the most powerful factor when considering the sign of the Scales.

What matters most to you is balance, which is probably not at all surprising considering what your zodiac sign actually means. Because of this you would go to tremendous lengths to make sure that your inner resolves create the right external signs and actions to offer the peace that you are looking for most of all.

Like most people born under the Air signs you are not quite as confident as you sometimes appear to be. In the main you are modest and not given to boasting, so you don't attract quite the level of attention of your fellow Air signs, Gemini and Aquarius. All the same you are quite capable of putting on an act when it's necessary to give a good account of yourself in public. You could be quaking inside but you do have the ability to hide this from the world at large.

Librans exhibit such a strong desire to be kind to everyone they meet that they may hide their inner feelings from some people altogether. It's important to remember to be basically honest, even if that means upsetting others a little. This is the most difficult trait for Libra to deal with and may go part of the way to explaining why so many relationship break-ups occur for people born under this zodiac sign. However, as long as you find ways and means to explain your deepest emotional needs, at least to those you love, all should be well.

In most respects you tend to be an open book, particularly to those who take the trouble to look. Your nature is not over-deep, and you are almost certainly not on some secret search to find the 'real you'. Although Libra is sometimes accused of being superficial there are many people in the world who would prefer simplicity to complications and duplicity.

Making the best of yourself

This may be the easiest category by far for the zodiac sign of Libra. The fact is that you rarely do anything else but offer the best version of what you are. Presentation is second nature to Libra, which just loves to be noticed. Despite this you are naturally modest and so not inclined to go over the top in company. You can be relied upon to say and do the right things for most of the time. Even when you consider your actions to be zany and perhaps less acceptable, this is not going to be the impression that the majority of people would get.

In a work sense you need to be involved in some sort of occupation that is clean, allows for a sense of order and ultimately offers the ability to use your head as well as your hands. The fact is that you don't care too much for unsavoury sorts of work and need to be in an environment that suits your basically refined nature. If the circumstances are right you can give a great deal to your work and will go far. Librans also need to be involved with others because they are natural co-operators. For this reason you may not be at your best when working alone or in situations that necessitate all the responsibilities being exclusively yours.

When in the social mainstream you tend to make the best of yourself by simply being what you naturally are. You don't need frills and fancies. Libra is able to make the best sort of impression by using the natural qualities inherent in the sign. As a result, your natural poise, your ability to cut through social divisions, your intelligence and your adaptability should all ensure that you remain popular.

What may occasionally prove difficult is being quite as dominant as the world assumes you ought to be. Many people equate efficiency with power. This is not the way of people born under the Scales, and you need to make that fact plain to anyone who seems to have the desire to shape you.

The impressions you give

Although the adage 'what you see is what you get' may be truer for Libra than for any of its companion signs, it can't be exclusively the case. However, under almost all circumstances you are likely to make friends. You are a much shrewder operator than sometimes appears to be the case and tend to weigh things in the balance very carefully. Libra can be most things to most people, and that's the sort of adaptability that ensures success at both a social and a professional level.

The chances are that you are already well respected and deeply liked by most of the people you know. This isn't so surprising since you are not inclined to make waves of any sort. Whether or not this leads to you achieving the degree of overall success that you deserve in life is quite a different matter. When impressions count you don't tend to let yourself down, or the people who rely on you. Adapting yourself to suit different circumstances is the meat and drink of your basic nature and you have plenty of poise and charm to disarm even the most awkward of people.

In affairs of the heart you are equally adept at putting others at their ease. There is very little difficulty involved in getting people to show their affection for you and when it comes to romance you are one of the most successful practitioners to be found anywhere. The only slight problem in this area of life, as with others, is that you are so talented at offering people what they want that you might not always be living the sort of life that genuinely suits you. Maybe giving the right impression is a little too important for Libra. A deeper form of honesty from the start would prevent you from having to show a less charming side to your nature in the end.

In most circumstances you can be relied upon to exhibit a warm, affectionate, kind, sincere and interesting face to the world at large. As long as this underpins truthfulness it's hard to understand how Libra could really go far wrong.

The way forward

You must already be fairly confident that you have the necessary skills and natural abilities to get on well in a world that is also filled with other people. From infancy most Librans learn how to rub along with others, whilst offering every indication that they are both adaptable and amenable to change. Your chameleon-like ability to 'change colour' in order to suit prevailing circumstances means that you occasionally drop back to being part of the wallpaper in the estimation of at least some people. A greater ability to make an impression probably would not go amiss sometimes, but making a big fuss isn't your way and you actively seek an uncomplicated sort of life.

Balance is everything to Libra, a fact that means there are times when you end up with nothing at all. What needs to be remembered is that there are occasions when everyone simply has to make a decision. This is the hardest thing in the world for you to do but when you manage it you become even more noticed by the world at large.

There's no doubt that people generally hold you in great affection. They know you to be quite capable and love your easy-going attitude to life. You are rarely judgmental and tend to offer almost anyone the benefit of the doubt. Although you are chatty, and inclined to listen avidly to gossip, it isn't your natural way to be unkind, caustic or backbiting. As a result it would seem that you have all the prerequisites to live an extremely happy life. Alas, things are rarely quite that easy.

It is very important for you to demonstrate to yourself, as well as to others, that you are an individual with thoughts and feelings of your own. So often do you defer to the needs of those around you that the real you gets somewhat squashed on the way. There have to be times when you are willing to say 'yes' or 'no' unequivocally, instead of a noncommittal 'I don't really mind' or 'whatever you think best'. At the end of the day you do have opinions and can lead yourself into the path of some severe frustrations if you are unwilling to voice them in the first place.

Try to be particularly honest in deep, emotional attachments. Many Libran relationships come to grief simply because there isn't enough earthy honesty present in the first place. People knowing how you feel won't make them care for you any less. A fully integrated, truthful Libran, with a willingness to participate in the decision making, turns out to be the person who is both successful and happy.

LIBRA ON THE CUSP

A strological profiles are altered for those people born at either the beginning or the end of a zodiac sign, or, more properly, on the cusps of a sign. In the case of Libra this would be on the 24th of September and for two or three days after, and similarly at the end of the sign, probably from the 21st to the 23rd of October.

The Virgo Cusp – September 24th to 26th

Here we find a Libran subject with a greater than average sense of responsibility and probably a better potential for success than is usually the case for Libra when taken alone. The Virgoan tendency to take itself rather too seriously is far less likely when the sign is mixed with Libra and the resultant nature is often deeply inspiring, and yet quite centred. The Virgo-cusp Libran has what it takes to break through the red tape of society, and yet can understand the need for its existence in the first place. You are caring and concerned, quick on the uptake and very ready to listen to any point of view but, at the end of the day, you know when it is going to be necessary to take a personal stance and this you are far more willing to do than would be the case for non-cuspid Librans.

Family members are important to you, but you always allow them their own individuality and won't get in the way of their personal need to spread their own wings, even at times when it's hard to take this positive stance. Practically speaking, you are a good home-maker but you also enjoy travelling and can benefit greatly from seeing the way other cultures think and behave. It is true that you can have the single-mindedness of a Virgoan, but even this aspect is modified by the Libran within you, so that you usually try to see alternative points of view and often succeed in doing so.

At work you really come into your own. Not only are you capable enough to deal with just about any eventuality, you are also willing to be flexible and to make up your mind instantly when it proves necessary to do so. Colleagues and subordinates alike tend to trust you. You may consider self-employment, unlike most Librans who are usually very worried by this prospect. Making your way in life is something you tend to take for granted, even when the going gets tough.

What people most like about you is that, despite your tremendously practical approach to life, you can be very zany and retain a sense of fun that is, at its best, second to none. Few people find you difficult to understand or to get on with in a day-to-day sense.

The Scorpio Cusp – October 21st to 23rd

The main difference between this cusp and the one at the Virgo end of Libra, is that you tend to be more emotionally motivated and of a slightly less practical nature. Routines are easy for you to address, though you can become very restless and tend to find your own emotional responses difficult to deal with. Sometimes even you don't understand what makes you tick, and that can be a problem. Actually you are not as complicated as you may have come to believe. It's simply that you have a unique view of life and one that doesn't always match that of the people around you, but as Libra instinctively wants to conform, this can lead to some personal confusion.

In family matters you are responsible, very caring and deeply committed to others. It's probable that you work in some field that finds you in direct contact with the public at large and many Scorpio-cusp Librans choose welfare, social or hospital work as a first choice. When it comes to love, you are flexible in your choice and the necessary attributes to promote a long-lasting and happy relationship are clearly present in your basic nature. If there are problems, they may come about as a result of your inability to choose properly in the first place, because you are the first to offer anyone the benefit of the doubt.

When it comes to the practicalities of life, Scorpio can prove to be extremely useful. It offers an 'edge' to your nature and, as Scorpio is a Fixed sign, you are less likely to lose ground because of lack of confidence than Libra alone would be. Your future can be bright, but only if you are willing to get involved in something that really interests you in the first place. You certainly do not care for getting your hands dirty and tend to gravitate towards more refined positions.

Creative potential is good and you could be very artistic, though if this extends to fine art, at least some of your pictures will have 'dark' overtones that might shock some people, including yourself. At base you are kind, caring, complicated, yet inspiring.

LIBRA AND ITS ASCENDANTS

The nature of every individual on the planet is composed of the rich variety of zodiac signs and planetary positions that were present at the time of their birth. Your Sun sign, which in your case is Libra, is one of the many factors when it comes to assessing the unique person you are. Probably the most important consideration, other than your Sun sign, is to establish the zodiac sign that was rising over the eastern horizon at the time that you were born. This is your Ascending or Rising sign. Most popular astrology fails to take account of the Ascendant, and yet its importance remains with you from the very moment of your birth, through every day of your life. The Ascendant is evident in the way you approach the world, and so, when meeting a person for the first time, it is this astrological influence that you are most likely to notice first. Our Ascending sign essentially represents what we appear to be, while the Sun sign is what we feel inside ourselves.

The Ascendant also has the potential for modifying our overall nature. For example, if you were born at a time of day when Libra was passing over the eastern horizon (this would be around the time of dawn) then you would be classed as a double Libran. As such, you would typify this zodiac sign, both internally and in your dealings with others. However, if your Ascendant sign turned out to be a Water sign, such as Pisces, there would be a profound alteration of nature, away from the expected qualities of Libra.

One of the reasons why popular astrology often ignores the Ascendant is that it has always been rather difficult to establish. We have found a way to make this possible by devising an easy-to-use table, which you will find on page 157 of this book. Using this, you can establish your Ascendant sign at a glance. You will need to know your rough time of birth, then it is simply a case of following the instructions.

For those readers who have no idea of their time of birth it might be worth allowing a good friend, or perhaps your partner, to read through the section that follows this introduction. Someone who deals with you on a regular basis may easily discover your Ascending sign, even though you could have some difficulty establishing it for yourself. A good understanding of this component of your nature is essential if you want to be aware of that 'other person' who is responsible for the way you make contact with the world at large. Your Sun sign, Ascendant sign, and the other pointers in this book

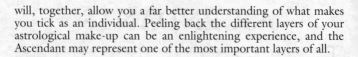

will, together, allow you a far better understanding of what makes you tick as an individual. Peeling back the different layers of your astrological make-up can be an enlightening experience, and the Ascendant may represent one of the most important layers of all.

Libra with Libra Ascendant

There is no doubt that you carry the very best of all Libran worlds in your nature, though at the same time there is a definite possibility that you often fall between two stools. The literal advice as a result is that you must sometimes make a decision, even though it isn't all that easy for you to do so. Not everyone understands your easy-going side and there are occasions when you could appear to be too flippant for your own good.

The way you approach the world makes you popular, and there is no doubt at all that you are the most diplomatic person to be found anywhere in the length and breadth of the zodiac. It is your job in life to stop people disagreeing and since you can always see every point of view, you make a good impression on the way.

Relationships can sometimes be awkward for you because you can change your mind so easily. But love is never lacking and you can be fairly certain of a generally happy life. Over-indulging is always a potential problem for Air-sign people such as yourself, and there are times in your life when you must get the rest and relaxation which is so important in funding a strong nervous system. Drink plenty of water to flush out a system that can be over-high in natural salts.

Libra with Scorpio Ascendant

There is some tendency for you to be far more deep than the average Libran would appear to be, and for this reason it is crucial that you lighten up from time to time. Every person with a Scorpio quality needs to remember that there is a happy and carefree side to all events, and your Libran quality should allow you to bear this in mind. Sometimes you try to do too many things at the same time. This is fine if you take the casual overview of Libra, but less sensible when you insist on picking the last bone out of every potential, as is much more the case for Scorpio.

When worries come along, as they sometimes will, be able to listen to what your friends have to say and also realise that they are more than willing to work on your behalf, if only because you are so loyal to them. You do have a quality of self-deception, but this should not get in the way too much if you combine the instinctive actions of Libra with the deep intuition of your Scorpio component.

Probably the most important factor of this combination is your ability to succeed in a financial sense. You make a good manager, but not of the authoritarian sort. Jobs in the media or where you are expected to make up your mind quickly would suit you because there is always an underpinning of practical sense that rarely lets you down.

Libra with Sagittarius Ascendant

A very happy combination this, with a great desire for life in all its forms and a need to push forward the bounds of the possible in a way that few other zodiac sign connections would do. You don't like the unpleasant or ugly in life and yet you are capable of dealing with both if you have to. Giving so much to humanity, you still manage to retain a degree of individuality that would surprise many, charm others, and please all.

On the reverse side of the same coin you might find that you are sometimes accused of being fickle, but this is only an expression of your need for change and variety, which is endemic to both these signs. True, you have more of a temper than would be the case for Libra when taken on its own, but such incidents would see you up and down in a flash, and it is almost impossible for you to bear a grudge of any sort. Routines get on your nerves and you are far happier when you can please yourself and get ahead at your own pace, which is quite fast.

As a lover you can make a big impression and most of you will not go short of affection in the early days, before you choose to commit yourself. Once you do, there is always a chance of romantic problems, but these are less likely when you have chosen carefully in the first place.

Libra with Capricorn Ascendant

It is a fact that Libra is the most patient of the Air signs, though like the others it needs to get things done fairly quickly. Capricorn, on the other hand, will work long and hard to achieve its objectives and will not be thwarted in the end. As a result this is a quite powerful sign combination and one that should lead to ultimate success.

Capricorn is often accused of taking itself too seriously and yet it has an ironic and really very funny sense of humour which only its chief confidants recognise. Libra is lighthearted, always willing to have fun and quite anxious to please. When these two basic types come together in their best forms, you might find yourself to be one of the most well- balanced people around. Certainly you know what you want, but you don't have to use a bulldozer in order to get it.

Active and enthusiastic when something really takes your fancy, you might also turn out to be one of the very best lovers of them all. The reason for this is that you have the depth of Capricorn but the lighter and more directly affectionate qualities of the Scales. What you want from life in a personal sense, you eventually tend to get, but you don't care too much if this takes you a while. Few people could deny that you are a faithful friend, a happy sort and a deeply magnetic personality.

Libra with Aquarius Ascendant

Stand by for a truly interesting and very inspiring combination here, but one that is sometimes rather difficult to fathom, even for the sort of people who believe themselves to be very perceptive. The reason for this could be that any situation has to be essentially fixed and constant in order to get a handle on it, and this is certainly not the case for the Aquarian–Libran type. The fact is that both these signs are Air signs, and to a certain extent as unpredictable as the wind itself.

To most people you seem to be original, frank, free and very outspoken. Not everything you do makes sense to others, and if you were alive during the hippy era, it is likely that you went around with flowers in your hair, for you are a free-thinking idealist at heart. With age you mature somewhat, but never too much, because you will always see the strange, the comical and the original in life. This is what keeps you young and is one of the factors that makes you so very attractive to members of the opposite sex. Many people will want to 'adopt' you, and you are at your very best when in company.

Much of your effort is expounded on others and yet, unless you discipline yourself a good deal, personal relationships of the romantic sort can bring certain difficulties. Careful planning is necessary.

Libra with Pisces Ascendant

An Air and Water combination, you are not easy to understand and have depths that show at times, surprising those people who thought they already knew what you were. You will always keep people guessing and are just as likely to hitchhike around Europe as you are to hold down a steady job, both of which you would undertake with the same degree of commitment and success. Usually young at heart, but always carrying the potential for an old head on young shoulders, you are something of a paradox and not at all easy for totally 'straight' types to understand. But you always make an impression and tend to be very attractive to members of the opposite sex.

In matters of health you do have to be a little careful because you dissipate much nervous energy and can sometimes be inclined to push yourself too hard, at least in a mental sense. Frequent periods of rest and meditation will do you the world of good and should improve your level of wisdom, which tends to be fairly high already. Much of your effort in life is expounded on behalf of humanity as a whole, for you care deeply, love totally and always give of your best. Whatever your faults and failings might be, you are one of the most popular people around.

Libra with Aries Ascendant

Libra has the tendency to bring out the best in any zodiac sign, and this is no exception when it comes together with Aries. You may, in fact, be the most comfortable of all Aries types, simply because Libra tempers some of your more assertive qualities and gives you the chance to balance out opposing forces, both inside yourself and in the world outside. You are fun to be with and make the staunchest friend possible. Although you are generally affable, few people would try to put one over on you because they would quickly come to know how far you are willing to go before you let forth a string of invective that would shock those who previously underestimated your basic Aries traits.

Home and family are very dear to you, but you are more tolerant than some Aries types are inclined to be and you have a youthful zest for life that should stay with you no matter what age you manage to achieve. There is always something interesting to do and your mind is a constant stream of possibilities. This makes you very creative and you may also demonstrate a desire to look good at all times. You may not always be quite as confident as you appear to be, but few would guess the fact.

Libra with Taurus Ascendant

A fortunate combination in many ways, this is a double-Venus rulership, since both Taurus and Libra are heavily reliant on the planet of love. You are social, amiable and a natural diplomat, anxious to please and ready to care for just about anyone who shows interest in you. You hate disorder, which means that there is a place for everything and everything in its place. This can throw up the odd paradox however, since being half Libran you cannot always work out where that place ought to be! You deal with life in a humorous way and are quite capable of seeing the absurd in yourself, as well as in others. Your heart is no bigger than that of the quite typical Taurean, but it sits rather closer to the surface and so others recognise it more.

On those occasions when you know you are standing on firm ground you can show great confidence, even if you have to be ready to change some of your opinions at the drop of a hat. When this happens you can be quite at odds with yourself, because Taurus doesn't take very many U-turns, whereas Libra does. Don't expect to know yourself too well, and keep looking for the funny side of things, because it is within humour that you forge the sort of life that suits you best.

♎

Libra with Gemini Ascendant

What a happy-go-lucky soul you are and how popular you tend to be with those around you. Libra is, like Gemini, an Air sign and this means that you are the communicator par excellence, even by Gemini standards. It can sometimes be difficult for you to make up your mind about things because Libra does not exactly aid this process, and especially not when it is allied to Mercurial Gemini. Frequent periods of deep thought are necessary, and meditation would do you a great deal of good. All the same, although you might sometimes be rather unsure of yourself, you are rarely without a certain balance. Clean and tidy surroundings suit you the best, though this is far from easy to achieve because you are invariably dashing off to some place or other, so you really need someone to sort things out in your absence.

The most important fact of all is that you are much loved by your friends, of which there are likely to be very many. Because you are so willing to help them out, in return they are usually there when it matters and they would probably go to almost any length on your behalf. You exhibit a fine sense of justice and will usually back those in trouble. Charities tend to be attractive to you and you do much on behalf of those who live on the fringes of society or people who are truly alone.

Libra with Cancer Ascendant

What an absolutely pleasant and approachable sort of person you are, and how much you have to offer. Like most people associated with the sign of Cancer you give yourself freely to the world, and will always be on hand if anyone is in trouble or needs the special touch you can bring to almost any problem. Behaving in this way is the biggest part of what you are and so people come to rely on you very heavily. Like Libra you can see both sides of any coin and you exhibit the Libran tendency to jump about from one foot to the other when it is necessary to make decisions relating to your own life. This is not usually the case when you are dealing with others however, because the cooler and more detached qualities of Cancer will show through in these circumstances.

It would be fair to say that you do not deal with routines as well as Cancer alone might do and you need a degree of variety in your life, which in your case often comes in the form of travel, which can be distant and of long duration. It isn't unusual for people who have this zodiac combination to end up living abroad, though even this does little to prevent you from getting itchy feet from time to time. In romance you show an original quality that keeps the relationship young and working very well.

Libra with Leo Ascendant

Libra brings slightly more flexibility to the fixed quality of the Leo nature. On the whole you do not represent a picture that is so much different from other versions of the Lion, though you find more time to smile, enjoy changing your mind a great deal more and have a greater number of casual friends. Few would find you proud or haughty and you retain the common touch that can be so important when it comes to getting on in life generally. At work you like to do something that brings variety, and would probably soon tire of doing the same task over and over again. Many of you are teachers, for you have patience, allied to a stubborn core. This can be an indispensable combination on occasions and is part of the reason for the material success that many folk with this combination of signs achieve.

It isn't often that you get down in the dumps, after all there is generally something more important around the next corner, and you love the cut and thrust of everyday life. You always manage to stay young at heart, no matter what your age might be, and you revel in the company of interesting and stimulating types. Maybe you should try harder to concentrate on one thing at once and also strive to retain a serious opinion for more than ten minutes at a time. However, Leo helps to control your flighty tendencies.

Libra with Virgo Ascendant

Libra has the ability to lighten almost any load, and it is particularly good at doing so when it is brought together with the much more repressed sign of Virgo. To the world at large you seem relaxed, happy and able to cope with most of the pressures that life places upon you. Not only do you deal with your own life in a bright and breezy manner but you are usually on hand to help others out of any dilemma that they might make for themselves. With excellent powers of communication, you leave the world at large in no doubt whatsoever concerning both your opinions and your wishes. It is in the talking stakes that you really excel because Virgo brings the silver tongue of Mercury and Libra adds the Air-sign desire to be in constant touch with the world outside your door.

You like to have a good time and can often be found in the company of interesting and stimulating people, who have the ability to bring out the very best in your bright and sparkling personality. Underneath however, there is still much of the worrying Virgoan to be found and this means that you have to learn to relax inside as well as appearing to do so externally. In fact you are much more complex than most people would realise, and definitely would not be suited to a life that allowed you too much time to think about yourself.

THE MOON AND THE PART IT PLAYS IN YOUR LIFE

In astrology the Moon is probably the single most important heavenly body after the Sun. Its unique position, as partner to the Earth on its journey around the solar system, means that the Moon appears to pass through the signs of the zodiac extremely quickly. The zodiac position of the Moon at the time of your birth plays a great part in personal character and is especially significant in the build-up of your emotional nature.

Your Own Moon Sign

Discovering the position of the Moon at the time of your birth has always been notoriously difficult because tracking the complex zodiac positions of the Moon is not easy. This process has been reduced to three simple stages with our Lunar Tables. A breakdown of the Moon's zodiac positions can be found from page 35 onwards, so that once you know what your Moon Sign is, you can see what part this plays in the overall build-up of your personal character.

If you follow the instructions on the next page you will soon be able to work out exactly what zodiac sign the Moon occupied on the day that you were born and you can then go on to compare the reading for this position with those of your Sun sign and your Ascendant. It is partly the comparison between these three important positions that goes towards making you the unique individual you are.

HOW TO DISCOVER YOUR MOON SIGN

This is a three-stage process. You may need a pen and a piece of paper but if you follow the instructions below the process should only take a minute or so.

STAGE 1 First of all you need to know the Moon Age at the time of your birth. If you look at Moon Table 1, on page 33, you will find all the years between 1920 and 2018 down the left side. Find the year of your birth and then trace across to the right to the month of your birth. Where the two intersect you will find a number. This is the date of the New Moon in the month that you were born. You now need to count forward the number of days between the New Moon and your own birthday. For example, if the New Moon in the month of your birth was shown as being the 6th and you were born on the 20th, your Moon Age Day would be 14. If the New Moon in the month of your birth came after your birthday, you need to count forward from the New Moon in the previous month. Whatever the result, jot this number down so that you do not forget it.

STAGE 2 Take a look at Moon Table 2 on page 34. Down the left hand column look for the date of your birth. Now trace across to the month of your birth. Where the two meet you will find a letter. Copy this letter down alongside your Moon Age Day.

STAGE 3 Moon Table 3 on page 34 will supply you with the zodiac sign the Moon occupied on the day of your birth. Look for your Moon Age Day down the left hand column and then for the letter you found in Stage 2. Where the two converge you will find a zodiac sign and this is the sign occupied by the Moon on the day that you were born.

Your Zodiac Moon Sign Explained

You will find a profile of all zodiac Moon Signs on pages 35 to 38, showing in yet another way how astrology helps to make you into the individual that you are. In each daily entry of the Astral Diary you can find the zodiac position of the Moon for every day of the year. This also allows you to discover your lunar birthdays. Since the Moon passes through all the signs of the zodiac in about a month, you can expect something like twelve lunar birthdays each year. At these times you are likely to be emotionally steady and able to make the sort of decisions that have real, lasting value.

MOON TABLE 1

YEAR	AUG	SEP	OCT	YEAR	AUG	SEP	OCT	YEAR	AUG	SEP	OCT
1920	14	12	12	1953	9	8	8	1986	5	4	3
1921	3	2	1/30	1954	28	27	26	1987	24	23	22
1922	22	21	20	1955	17	16	15	1988	12	11	10
1923	12	10	10	1956	6	4	4	1989	1/31	29	29
1924	30	28	28	1957	25	23	23	1990	20	19	18
1925	19	18	17	1958	15	13	12	1991	9	8	8
1926	8	7	6	1959	4	3	2/31	1992	28	26	25
1927	27	25	25	1960	22	21	20	1993	17	16	15
1928	16	14	14	1961	11	10	9	1994	7	5	5
1929	5	3	2	1962	30	28	28	1995	26	24	24
1930	24	22	20	1963	19	17	17	1996	14	13	11
1931	13	12	11	1964	7	6	5	1997	3	2	2/31
1932	2/31	30	29	1965	26	25	24	1998	22	20	20
1933	21	19	19	1966	16	14	14	1999	11	10	8
1934	10	9	8	1967	5	4	3	2000	29	27	27
1935	29	27	27	1968	24	23	22	2001	19	17	17
1936	17	15	15	1969	12	11	10	2002	8	6	6
1937	6	4	4	1970	2	1	1/30	2003	27	26	25
1938	25	23	23	1971	20	19	19	2004	14	13	12
1939	15	13	12	1972	9	8	8	2005	4	3	2
1940	4	2	1/30	1973	28	27	26	2006	23	22	21
1941	22	21	20	1974	17	16	15	2007	13	12	11
1942	12	10	10	1975	7	5	5	2008	1/31	30	29
1943	1/30	29	29	1976	25	23	23	2009	20	19	18
1944	18	17	17	1977	14	13	12	2010	10	8	8
1945	8	6	6	1978	4	2	2/31	2011	29	27	27
1946	26	25	24	1979	22	21	20	2012	17	16	15
1947	16	14	14	1980	11	10	9	2013	6	4	4
1948	5	3	2	1981	29	28	27	2014	24	23	22
1949	24	23	21	1982	19	17	17	2015	15	13	12
1950	13	12	11	1983	8	7	6	2016	2	1	30
1951	2	1	1/30	1984	26	25	24	2017	22	20	20
1952	20	19	18	1985	16	14	14	2018	11	9	9

TABLE 2   MOON TABLE 3

DAY	SEP	OCT	M/D	X	Y	Z	a	b	d	e
1	X	a	0	VI	VI	LI	LI	LI	LI	SC
2	X	a	1	VI	LI	LI	LI	LI	SC	SC
3	X	a	2	LI	LI	LI	LI	SC	SC	SC
4	Y	b	3	LI	LI	SC	SC	SC	SC	SA
5	Y	b	4	LI	SC	SC	SC	SA	SA	SA
6	Y	b	5	SC	SC	SC	SA	SA	SA	CP
7	Y	b	6	SC	SA	SA	SA	CP	CP	CP
8	Y	b	7	SA	SA	SA	SA	CP	CP	AQ
9	Y	b	8	SA	SA	CP	CP	CP	CP	AQ
10	Y	b	9	SA	CP	CP	CP	AQ	AQ	AQ
11	Y	b	10	CP	CP	CP	AQ	AQ	AQ	PI
12	Y	b	11	CP	AQ	AQ	AQ	PI	PI	PI
13	Y	b	12	AQ	AQ	AQ	PI	PI	PI	AR
14	Z	d	13	AQ	AQ	PI	PI	AR	PI	AR
15	Z	d	14	PI	PI	PI	AR	AR	AR	TA
16	Z	d	15	PI	PI	PI	AR	AR	AR	TA
17	Z	d	16	PI	AR	AR	AR	AR	TA	TA
18	Z	d	17	AR	AR	AR	AR	TA	TA	GE
19	Z	d	18	AR	AR	AR	TA	TA	GE	GE
20	Z	d	19	AR	TA	TA	TA	TA	GE	GE
21	Z	d	20	TA	TA	TA	GE	GE	GE	CA
22	Z	d	21	TA	GE	GE	GE	GE	CA	CA
23	Z	d	22	GE	GE	GE	GE	CA	CA	CA
24	a	e	23	GE	GE	GE	CA	CA	CA	LE
25	a	e	24	GE	CA	CA	CA	CA	LE	LE
26	a	e	25	CA	CA	CA	CA	LE	LE	LE
27	a	e	26	CA	LE	LE	LE	LE	VI	VI
28	a	e	27	LE	LE	LE	LE	VI	VI	VI
29	a	e	28	LE	LE	LE	VI	VI	VI	LI
30	a	e	29	LE	VI	VI	VI	VI	LI	LI
31	–	e								

AR = Aries, TA = Taurus, GE = Gemini, CA = Cancer, LE = Leo, VI = Virgo,
LI = Libra, SC = Scorpio, SA = Sagittarius, CP = Capricorn, AQ = Aquarius, PI = Pisces

MOON SIGNS

Moon in Aries

You have a strong imagination, courage, determination and a desire to do things in your own way and forge your own path through life.

Originality is a key attribute; you are seldom stuck for ideas although your mind is changeable and you could take the time to focus on individual tasks. Often quick-tempered, you take orders from few people and live life at a fast pace. Avoid health problems by taking regular time out for rest and relaxation.

Emotionally, it is important that you talk to those you are closest to and work out your true feelings. Once you discover that people are there to help, there is less necessity for you to do everything yourself.

Moon in Taurus

The Moon in Taurus gives you a courteous and friendly manner, which means you are likely to have many friends.

The good things in life mean a lot to you, as Taurus is an Earth sign that delights in experiences which please the senses. Hence you are probably a lover of good food and drink, which may in turn mean you need to keep an eye on the bathroom scales, especially as looking good is also important to you.

Emotionally you are fairly stable and you stick by your own standards. Taureans do not respond well to change. Intuition also plays an important part in your life.

Moon in Gemini

You have a warm-hearted character, sympathetic and eager to help others. At times reserved, you can also be articulate and chatty: this is part of the paradox of Gemini, which always brings duplicity to the nature. You are interested in current affairs, have a good intellect, and are good company and likely to have many friends. Most of your friends have a high opinion of you and would be ready to defend you should the need arise. However, this is usually unnecessary, as you are quite capable of defending yourself in any verbal confrontation.

Travel is important to your inquisitive mind and you find intellectual stimulus in mixing with people from different cultures. You also gain much from reading, writing and the arts but you do need plenty of rest and relaxation in order to avoid fatigue.

Moon in Cancer

The Moon in Cancer at the time of birth is a fortunate position as Cancer is the Moon's natural home. This means that the qualities of compassion and understanding given by the Moon are especially enhanced in your nature, and you are friendly and sociable and cope well with emotional pressures. You cherish home and family life, and happily do the domestic tasks. Your surroundings are important to you and you hate squalor and filth. You are likely to have a love of music and poetry.

Your basic character, although at times changeable like the Moon itself, depends on symmetry. You aim to make your surroundings comfortable and harmonious, for yourself and those close to you.

Moon in Leo

The best qualities of the Moon and Leo come together to make you warm-hearted, fair, ambitious and self-confident. With good organisational abilities, you invariably rise to a position of responsibility in your chosen career. This is fortunate as you don't enjoy being an 'also-ran' and would rather be an important part of a small organisation than a menial in a large one.

You should be lucky in love, and happy, provided you put in the effort to make a comfortable home for yourself and those close to you. It is likely that you will have a love of pleasure, sport, music and literature. Life brings you many rewards, most of them as a direct result of your own efforts, although you may be luckier than average and ready to make the best of any situation.

Moon in Virgo

You are endowed with good mental abilities and a keen receptive memory, but you are never ostentatious or pretentious. Naturally quite reserved, you still have many friends, especially of the opposite sex. Marital relationships must be discussed carefully and worked at so that they remain harmonious, as personal attachments can be a problem if you do not give them your full attention.

Talented and persevering, you possess artistic qualities and are a good homemaker. Earning your honours through genuine merit, you work long and hard towards your objectives but show little pride in your achievements. Many short journeys will be undertaken in your life.

Moon in Libra

With the Moon in Libra you are naturally popular and make friends easily. People like you, probably more than you realise, you bring fun to a party and are a natural diplomat. For all its good points, Libra is not the most stable of astrological signs and, as a result, your emotions can be a little unstable too. Therefore, although the Moon in Libra is said to be good for love and marriage, your Sun sign and Rising sign will have an important effect on your emotional and loving qualities.

You must remember to relate to others in your decision-making. Co-operation is crucial because Libra represents the 'balance' of life that can only be achieved through harmonious relationships. Conformity is not easy for you because Libra, an Air sign, likes its independence.

Moon in Scorpio

Some people might call you pushy. In fact, all you really want to do is to live life to the full and protect yourself and your family from the pressures of life. Take care to avoid giving the impression of being sarcastic or impulsive and use your energies wisely and constructively.

You have great courage and you invariably achieve your goals by force of personality and sheer effort. You are fond of mystery and are good at predicting the outcome of situations and events. Travel experiences can be beneficial to you.

You may experience problems if you do not take time to examine your motives in a relationship, and also if you allow jealousy, always a feature of Scorpio, to cloud your judgement.

Moon in Sagittarius

The Moon in Sagittarius helps to make you a generous individual with humanitarian qualities and a kind heart. Restlessness may be intrinsic as your mind is seldom still. Perhaps because of this, you have a need for change that could lead you to several major moves during your adult life. You are not afraid to stand your ground when you know your judgement is right, you speak directly and have good intuition.

At work you are quick, efficient and versatile and so you make an ideal employee. You need work to be intellectually demanding and do not enjoy tedious routines.

In relationships, you anger quickly if faced with stupidity or deception, though you are just as quick to forgive and forget. Emotionally, there are times when your heart rules your head.

Moon in Capricorn

The Moon in Capricorn makes you popular and likely to come into the public eye in some way. The watery Moon is not entirely comfortable in the Earth sign of Capricorn and this may lead to some difficulties in the early years of life. An initial lack of creative ability and indecision must be overcome before the true qualities of patience and perseverance inherent in Capricorn can show through.

You have good administrative ability and are a capable worker, and if you are careful you can accumulate wealth. But you must be cautious and take professional advice in partnerships, as you are open to deception. You may be interested in social or welfare work, which suit your organisational skills and sympathy for others.

Moon in Aquarius

The Moon in Aquarius makes you an active and agreeable person with a friendly, easy-going nature. Sympathetic to the needs of others, you flourish in a laid-back atmosphere. You are broad-minded, fair and open to suggestion, although sometimes you have an unconventional quality which others can find hard to understand.

You are interested in the strange and curious, and in old articles and places. You enjoy trips to these places and gain much from them. Political, scientific and educational work interests you and you might choose a career in science or technology.

Money-wise, you make gains through innovation and concentration and Lunar Aquarians often tackle more than one job at a time. In love you are kind and honest.

Moon in Pisces

You have a kind, sympathetic nature, somewhat retiring at times, but you always take account of others' feelings and help when you can.

Personal relationships may be problematic, but as life goes on you can learn from your experiences and develop a better understanding of yourself and the world around you.

You have a fondness for travel, appreciate beauty and harmony and hate disorder and strife. You may be fond of literature and would make a good writer or speaker yourself. You have a creative imagination and may come across as an incurable romantic. You have strong intuition, maybe bordering on a mediumistic quality, which sets you apart from the mass. You may not be rich in cash terms, but your personal gifts are worth more than gold.

LIBRA IN LOVE

Discover how compatible you are with people from the same and other signs of the zodiac. Five stars equals a match made in heaven!

Libra meets Libra

This is a potentially successful match because Librans are extremely likeable people, and so it stands to reason that two Librans together will be twice as pleasant and twice as much fun. However, Librans can also be indecisive and need an anchor from which to find practical and financial success, and obviously one Libran won't provide this for another. Librans can be flighty in a romantic sense, so both parties will need to develop a steadfast approach for a long-term relationship. Star rating: ****

Libra meets Scorpio

Many astrologers have reservations about this match because, on the surface, the signs are so different. However, this couple may find fulfilment because these differences mean that their respective needs are met. Scorpio needs a partner to lighten the load which won't daunt Libra, while Libra looks for a steadfast quality which it doesn't possess, but Scorpio can supply naturally. Financial success is possible because they both have good ideas and back them up with hard work and determination. All in all, a promising outlook. Star rating: ****

Libra meets Sagittarius

Libra and Sagittarius are both adaptable signs who get on well with most people, but this promising outlook often does not follow through because each brings out the flighty side of the other. This combination is great for a fling, but when the romance is over someone needs to see to the practical side of life. Both signs are well meaning, pleasant and kind, but are either of them constant enough to build a life together? In at least some of the cases, the answer would be no. Star rating: ***

Libra meets Capricorn

Libra and Capricorn rub each other up the wrong way because their attitudes to life are so different, and although both are capable of doing something about this, in reality they probably won't. Capricorn is steady, determined and solid, while Libra is bright but sometimes superficial and not entirely reliable. They usually lack the instant spark needed to get them together in the first place, so when it does happen it is often because one of the partners is not typical of their sign. Star rating: **

Libra meets Aquarius

One of the best combinations imaginable, partly because both are Air signs and so share a common meeting point. But perhaps the more crucial factor is that both signs respect each other. Aquarius loves life and originality, and is quite intellectual. Libra is similar, but more balanced and rather less eccentric. A visit to this couple's house would be entertaining and full of zany wit, activity and excitement. Both are keen to travel and may prefer to 'find themselves' before taking on too many domestic responsibilities. Star rating: *****

Libra meets Pisces

Libra and Pisces can be extremely fond of each other, even deeply in love, but this alone isn't a stable foundation for long-term success. Pisces is extremely deep and doesn't even know itself very well. Libra may initially find this intriguing but will eventually feel frustrated at being unable to understand the Piscean's emotional and personal feelings. Pisces can be jealous and may find Libra's flightiness difficult, which Libra can't stand. They are great friends and they may make it to the romantic stakes, but when they get there a lot of effort will be necessary. Star rating: ***

Libra meets Aries

These are zodiac opposites which means a make-or-break situation. The match will either be a great success or a dismal failure. Why? Well, Aries finds it difficult to understand the flighty Air-sign tendencies of Libra, whilst the natural balance of Libra contradicts the unorthodox Arian methods. Any flexibility will come from Libra, which may mean that things work out for a while, but Libra only has so much patience and it may eventually run out. In the end, Aries may be just too bossy for an independent but sensitive sign like Libra. Star rating: **

Libra meets Taurus

A happy life is important to both these signs and, as they are both ruled by Venus, they share a common understanding, even though they display themselves so differently. Taurus is quieter than Libra, but can be decisive, and that's what counts. Libra is interested in absolutely everything, an infectious quality when seen through Taurean eyes. The slightly flighty qualities of Libra may lead to jealousy from the Bull. Not an argumentative relationship and one that often works well. There could be many changes of address for this pair. Star rating: ****

Libra meets Gemini

One of the best possible zodiac combinations. Libra and Gemini are both Air signs, which leads to a meeting of minds. Both signs simply love to have a good time, although Libra is the tidiest and less forgetful. Gemini's capricious nature won't bother Libra, who acts as a stabilising influence. Life should generally run smoothly, and any rows are likely to be short and sharp. Both parties genuinely like each other, which is of paramount importance in a relationship and, ultimately, there isn't a better reason for being or staying together. Star rating: *****

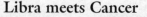

Libra meets Cancer

Almost anyone can get on with Libra, which is one of the most adaptable signs of them all. But being adaptable does not always lead to fulfilment and a successful match here will require a quiet Libran and a slightly more progressive Cancerian than the norm. Both signs are pleasant and polite, and like domestic order, but Libra may find Cancer too emotional and perhaps lacking in vibrancy, while Libra, on the other hand, may be a little too flighty for steady Cancer. Star rating: ***

Libra meets Leo

The biggest drawback here is likely to be in the issue of commitment. Leo knows everything about constancy and faithfulness, a lesson which, sadly, Libra needs to learn. Librans are easy-going and diplomatic, qualities which are useful when Leo is on the war-path. This couple should be compatible on a personal level and any problems tend to relate to the different way in which these signs deal with outside factors. With good will and an open mind, it can work out well enough. Star rating: ***

Libra meets Virgo

There have been some rare occasions when this match has found great success, but usually the darker and more inward-looking Virgoan depresses the naturally gregarious Libran. Libra appears self-confident, but is not so beneath the surface, and needs encouragement to develop inner confidence, which may not come from Virgo. Constancy can be a problem for Libra, who also tires easily and may find Virgo dull. A lighter, less serious approach to life from Virgo is needed to make this work. Star rating: **

VENUS:
THE PLANET OF LOVE

If you look up at the sky around sunset or sunrise you will often see Venus in close attendance to the Sun. It is arguably one of the most beautiful sights of all and there is little wonder that historically it became associated with the goddess of love. But although Venus does play an important part in the way you view love and in the way others see you romantically, this is only one of the spheres of influence that it enjoys in your overall character.

Venus has a part to play in the more cultured side of your life and has much to do with your appreciation of art, literature, music and general creativity. Even the way you look is responsive to the part of the zodiac that Venus occupied at the start of your life, though this fact is also down to your Sun sign and Ascending sign. If, at the time you were born, Venus occupied one of the more gregarious zodiac signs, you will be more likely to wear your heart on your sleeve, as well as to be more attracted to entertainment, social gatherings and good company. If on the other hand Venus occupied a quiet zodiac sign at the time of your birth, you would tend to be more retiring and less willing to shine in public situations.

It's good to know what part the planet Venus plays in your life for it can have a great bearing on the way you appear to the rest of the world and since we all have to mix with others, you can learn to make the very best of what Venus has to offer you.

One of the great complications in the past has always been trying to establish exactly what zodiac position Venus enjoyed when you were born because the planet is notoriously difficult to track. However, we have solved that problem by creating a table that is exclusive to your Sun sign, which you will find on the following page.

Establishing your Venus sign could not be easier. Just look up the year of your birth on the next page and you will see a sign of the zodiac. This was the sign that Venus occupied in the period covered by your sign in that year. If Venus occupied more than one sign during the period, this is indicated by the date on which the sign changed, and the name of the new sign. For instance, if you were born in 1950, Venus was in Virgo until the 4th October, after which time it was in Libra. If you were born before 4th October your Venus sign is Virgo, if you were born on or after 4th October, your Venus sign is Libra. Once you have established the position of Venus at the time of your birth, you can then look in the pages which follow to see how this has a bearing on your life as a whole.

1920 LIBRA / 30.9 SCORPIO
1921 LEO / 26.9 VIRGO /
   21.10 LIBRA
1922 SCORPIO / 11.10 SAGITTARIUS
1923 LIBRA / 16.10 SCORPIO
1924 LEO / 8.10 VIRGO
1925 SCORPIO / 12.10 SAGITTARIUS
1926 VIRGO / 6.10 LIBRA
1927 VIRGO
1928 LIBRA / 29.9 SCORPIO
1929 LEO / 26.9 VIRGO /
   20.10 LIBRA
1930 SCORPIO / 12.10 SAGITTARIUS
1931 LIBRA / 15.10 SCORPIO
1932 LEO / 7.10 VIRGO
1933 SCORPIO / 11.10 SAGITTARIUS
1934 VIRGO / 5.10 LIBRA
1935 VIRGO
1936 LIBRA / 28.9 SCORPIO
1937 LEO / 25.9 VIRGO /
   20.10 LIBRA
1938 SCORPIO / 14.10 SAGITTARIUS
1939 LIBRA / 14.10 SCORPIO
1940 LEO / 7.10 VIRGO
1941 SCORPIO / 11.10 SAGITTARIUS
1942 VIRGO / 5.10 LIBRA
1943 VIRGO
1944 LIBRA / 28.9 SCORPIO
1945 LEO / 25.9 VIRGO /
   19.10 LIBRA
1946 SCORPIO / 14.10 SAGITTARIUS
1947 LIBRA / 13.10 SCORPIO
1948 LEO / 7.10 VIRGO
1949 SCORPIO / 11.10 SAGITTARIUS
1950 VIRGO / 4.10 LIBRA
1951 VIRGO
1952 LIBRA / 27.9 SCORPIO
1953 VIRGO / 19.10 LIBRA
1954 SCORPIO / 16.10 SAGITTARIUS
1955 LIBRA / 12.10 SCORPIO
1956 LEO / 6.10 VIRGO
1957 SCORPIO / 10.10 SAGITTARIUS
1958 VIRGO / 4.10 LIBRA
1959 VIRGO / 28.9 LEO
1960 LIBRA / 27.9 SCORPIO
1961 VIRGO / 18.10 LIBRA
1962 SCORPIO / 16.10 SAGITTARIUS
1963 LIBRA / 12.10 SCORPIO
1964 LEO / 6.10 VIRGO
1965 SCORPIO / 9.10 SAGITTARIUS
1966 VIRGO / 4.10 LIBRA
1967 VIRGO / 3.10 LEO
1968 LIBRA / 26.9 SCORPIO
1969 VIRGO / 17.10 LIBRA

1970 SCORPIO / 19.10 SAGITTARIUS
1971 LIBRA / 11.10 SCORPIO
1972 LEO / 6.10 VIRGO
1973 SCORPIO / 9.10 SAGITTARIUS
1974 VIRGO / 3.10 LIBRA
1975 VIRGO / 5.10 LEO
1976 LIBRA / 26.9 SCORPIO
1977 VIRGO / 17.10 LIBRA
1978 SCORPIO / 19.10 SAGITTARIUS
1979 LIBRA / 11.10 SCORPIO
1980 LEO / 5.10 VIRGO
1981 SCORPIO / 9.10 SAGITTARIUS
1982 VIRGO / 3.10 LIBRA
1983 LEO / 7.10 VIRGO
1984 LIBRA / 25.9 SCORPIO
1985 VIRGO / 16.10 LIBRA
1986 SCORPIO
1987 LIBRA / 10.10 SCORPIO
1988 LEO / 5.10 VIRGO
1989 SCORPIO / 8.10 SAGITTARIUS
1990 VIRGO / 2.10 LIBRA
1991 VIRGO / 8.10 LEO
1992 LIBRA / 25.9 SCORPIO
1993 VIRGO / 16.10 LIBRA
1994 SCORPIO
1995 LIBRA / 10.10 SCORPIO
1996 LEO / 5.10 VIRGO
1997 SCORPIO / 8.10 SAGITTARIUS
1998 VIRGO / 2.10 LIBRA
1999 VIRGO / 9.10 LEO
2000 LIBRA / 25.9 SCORPIO
2001 LEO / 5.10 VIRGO
2002 SCORPIO / 8.10 SAGITTARIUS
2003 LIBRA / 10.10 SCORPIO
2004 LEO / 5.10 VIRGO
2005 SCORPIO / 8.10 SAGITTARIUS
2006 VIRGO / 2.10 LIBRA
2007 VIRGO / 9.10 LEO
2008 LIBRA / 25.9 SCORPIO
2009 LEO / 5.10 VIRGO
2010 SCORPIO / 8.10 SAGITTARIUS
2011 LIBRA / 10.10 SCORPIO
2012 LEO / 5.10 VIRGO
2013 SCORPIO / 8.10 SAGITTARIUS
2014 VIRGO / 2.10 LIBRA
2015 VIRGO / 9.10 LEO
2016 SCORPIO / 19.10 SAGITTARIUS
2017 LEO / 5.10 VIRGO
2018 SCORPIO / 8.10 SAGITTARIUS

VENUS THROUGH THE ZODIAC SIGNS

Venus in Aries

Amongst other things, the position of Venus in Aries indicates a fondness for travel, music and all creative pursuits. Your nature tends to be affectionate and you would try not to create confusion or difficulty for others if it could be avoided. Many people with this planetary position have a great love of the theatre, and mental stimulation is of the greatest importance. Early romantic attachments are common with Venus in Aries, so it is very important to establish a genuine sense of romantic continuity. Early marriage is not recommended, especially if it is based on sympathy. You may give your heart a little too readily on occasions.

Venus in Taurus

You are capable of very deep feelings and your emotions tend to last for a very long time. This makes you a trusting partner and lover, whose constancy is second to none. In life you are precise and careful and always try to do things the right way. Although this means an ordered life, which you are comfortable with, it can also lead you to be rather too fussy for your own good. Despite your pleasant nature, you are very fixed in your opinions and quite able to speak your mind. Others are attracted to you and historical astrologers always quoted this position of Venus as being very fortunate in terms of marriage. However, if you find yourself involved in a failed relationship, it could take you a long time to trust again.

Venus in Gemini

As with all associations related to Gemini, you tend to be quite versatile, anxious for change and intelligent in your dealings with the world at large. You may gain money from more than one source but you are equally good at spending it. There is an inference here that you are a good communicator, via either the written or the spoken word, and you love to be in the company of interesting people. Always on the look-out for culture, you may also be very fond of music, and love to indulge the curious and cultured side of your nature. In romance you tend to have more than one relationship and could find yourself associated with someone who has previously been a friend or even a distant relative.

Venus in Cancer

You often stay close to home because you are very fond of family and enjoy many of your most treasured moments when you are with those you love. Being naturally sympathetic, you will always do anything you can to support those around you, even people you hardly know at all. This charitable side of your nature is your most noticeable trait and is one of the reasons why others are naturally so fond of you. Being receptive and in some cases even psychic, you can see through to the soul of most of those with whom you come into contact. You may not commence too many romantic attachments but when you do give your heart, it tends to be unconditionally.

Venus in Leo

It must become quickly obvious to almost anyone you meet that you are kind, sympathetic and yet determined enough to stand up for anyone or anything that is truly important to you. Bright and sunny, you warm the world with your natural enthusiasm and would rarely do anything to hurt those around you, or at least not intentionally. In romance you are ardent and sincere, though some may find your style just a little overpowering. Gains come through your contacts with other people and this could be especially true with regard to romance, for love and money often come hand in hand for those who were born with Venus in Leo. People claim to understand you, though you are more complex than you seem.

Venus in Virgo

Your nature could well be fairly quiet no matter what your Sun sign might be, though this fact often manifests itself as an inner peace and would not prevent you from being basically sociable. Some delays and even the odd disappointment in love cannot be ruled out with this planetary position, though it's a fact that you will usually find the happiness you look for in the end. Catapulting yourself into romantic entanglements that you know to be rather ill-advised is not sensible, and it would be better to wait before you committed yourself exclusively to any one person. It is the essence of your nature to serve the world at large and through doing so it is possible that you will attract money at some stage in your life.

Venus in Libra

Venus is very comfortable in Libra and bestows upon those people who have this planetary position a particular sort of kindness that is easy to recognise. This is a very good position for all sorts of friendships and also for romantic attachments that usually bring much joy into your life. Few individuals with Venus in Libra would avoid marriage and since you are capable of great depths of love, it is likely that you will find a contented personal life. You like to mix with people of integrity and intelligence but don't take kindly to scruffy surroundings or work that means getting your hands too dirty. Careful speculation, good business dealings and money through marriage all seem fairly likely.

Venus in Scorpio

You are quite open and tend to spend money quite freely, even on those occasions when you don't have very much. Although your intentions are always good, there are times when you get yourself in to the odd scrape and this can be particularly true when it comes to romance, which you may come to late or from a rather unexpected direction. Certainly you have the power to be happy and to make others contented on the way, but you find the odd stumbling block on your journey through life and it could seem that you have to work harder than those around you. As a result of this, you gain a much deeper understanding of the true value of personal happiness than many people ever do, and are likely to achieve true contentment in the end.

Venus in Sagittarius

You are lighthearted, cheerful and always able to see the funny side of any situation. These facts enhance your popularity, which is especially high with members of the opposite sex. You should never have to look too far to find romantic interest in your life, though it is just possible that you might be too willing to commit yourself before you are certain that the person in question is right for you. Part of the problem here extends to other areas of life too. The fact is that you like variety in everything and so can tire of situations that fail to offer it. All the same, if you choose wisely and learn to understand your restless side, then great happiness can be yours.

Venus in Capricorn

The most notable trait that comes from Venus in this position is that it makes you trustworthy and able to take on all sorts of responsibilities in life. People are instinctively fond of you and love you all the more because you are always ready to help those who are in any form of need. Social and business popularity can be yours and there is a magnetic quality to your nature that is particularly attractive in a romantic sense. Anyone who wants a partner for a lover, a spouse and a good friend too would almost certainly look in your direction. Constancy is the hallmark of your nature and unfaithfulness would go right against the grain. You might sometimes be a little too trusting.

Venus in Aquarius

This location of Venus offers a fondness for travel and a desire to try out something new at every possible opportunity. You are extremely easy to get along with and tend to have many friends from varied backgrounds, classes and inclinations. You like to live a distinct sort of life and gain a great deal from moving about, both in a career sense and with regard to your home. It is not out of the question that you could form a romantic attachment to someone who comes from far away or be attracted to a person of a distinctly artistic and original nature. What you cannot stand is jealousy, for you have friends of both sexes and would want to keep things that way.

Venus in Pisces

The first thing people tend to notice about you is your wonderful, warm smile. Being very charitable by nature you will do anything to help others, even if you don't know them well. Much of your life may be spent sorting out situations for other people, but it is very important to feel that you are living for yourself too. In the main, you remain cheerful, and tend to be quite attractive to members of the opposite sex. Where romantic attachments are concerned, you could be drawn to people who are significantly older or younger than yourself or to someone with a unique career or point of view. It might be best for you to avoid marrying whilst you are still very young.

LIBRA:
2017 DIARY PAGES

October 2017

1 SUNDAY
Moon Age Day 11   Moon Sign Aquarius

This could be a very confusing and tense time as far as your personal life is concerned but only if you fail to look at things in an objective and honest manner. You could easily be worrying about something without any evidence or justification and that means dissipating otherwise useful energy to no real purpose.

2 MONDAY
Moon Age Day 12   Moon Sign Aquarius

An exciting and adventurous couple of days lie before you. There are some really good planetary influences, all of which are urging you onwards towards new incentives and activities. With no time to hang around you will be showing the world who is boss right now and few would stand in your way.

3 TUESDAY
Moon Age Day 13   Moon Sign Pisces

Progress in your career depends on your ability to think down completely new channels. Libra is certainly on the ball at the moment but there is a tendency for you to sometimes get stuck in your way of thinking. The more revolutionary you are at present, the greater is the chance that the world will take notice.

4 WEDNESDAY
Moon Age Day 14   Moon Sign Pisces

Your critical faculties are excellent and it would take someone very clever indeed to fool you at the moment. That makes this an ideal time for looking at and signing documents of any sort and for embarking on a new project that is going to demand a great deal of your time and attention in the weeks ahead.

5 THURSDAY   *Moon Age Day 15   Moon Sign Aries*

Basically the lunar low brings a slight downer and a time during which you might as well take a well-earned break. Not everything you do is going wrong but it will be hard to make any significant headway and it might be best not to push yourself. Colleagues will fill the breach for you and friends are supportive too.

6 FRIDAY   *Moon Age Day 16   Moon Sign Aries*

Today could be slightly characterised by confusion - that is unless you take one job at a time and think things through carefully before you commit yourself to anything at all. Fortunately there is likely to be a great deal of good humour about too, together with the company of people who have the ability to make you laugh out loud.

7 SATURDAY   *Moon Age Day 17   Moon Sign Taurus*

It is towards your friends that you tend to look for a good time this weekend. Formal situations are not significant and you may prefer to make up your mind as you go along when it comes to enjoyment. The more spontaneous you are, the greater is the chance that you encounter one of those very special times that cannot be planned.

8 SUNDAY   *Moon Age Day 18   Moon Sign Taurus*

Personal relationships and partnerships of all sorts can now bring much more than you bargained for, though generally in a very positive sense. Your powers of attraction are clearly very strong at the moment so don't be afraid to use them to your own advantage. Just don't lead someone up the garden path romantically.

9 MONDAY   *Moon Age Day 19   Moon Sign Taurus*

Romantic and social activities can represent a welcome diversion, especially since you are not in the mood to commit yourself exclusively to work. This would be an excellent time to bury the hatchet as far as a long-standing disagreement or row is concerned and you will also be playing the honest broker for others.

10 TUESDAY *Moon Age Day 20   Moon Sign Gemini*

You have a very fertile mind at the best of times but now it is truly active. Intuition is strong and you can afford to back your hunches to a much greater extent than has been the case in the very recent past. Life is now much more about feelings than evidence, though this might be hard for some Librans to appreciate.

11 WEDNESDAY *Moon Age Day 21   Moon Sign Gemini*

At this time the focus is clearly on your personal life and though you remain generally busy in a practical sense, much of your time is likely to be spent in the company of your partner, sorting things out and proving the depth of your affection. All this effort is certainly not wasted and there is great love coming back in your direction.

12 THURSDAY *Moon Age Day 22   Moon Sign Cancer*

Changes to your financial situation can give you more ease and comfort in your surroundings, though this is likely to be a gradual process that takes place over the next few weeks. For now you are likely to be happy. Libra is definitely in the mood for a spot of shopping or a trip to visit relatives or friends.

13 FRIDAY *Moon Age Day 23   Moon Sign Cancer*

You function well when it comes to looking after your own interests, especially in a financial sense. However it is quite important at the moment that you do not allow a sudden fondness for detail to get in your way at a time when a broad overview is far more useful. Colleagues should be very helpful around now.

14 SATURDAY *Moon Age Day 24   Moon Sign Leo*

People notice you this weekend, mainly because of the positive way you express yourself. It is easy to make others feel important and to encourage them to work hard on your behalf. Routines are not appealing and you long to ring the changes whenever it proves to be possible. A late holiday might be in order.

15 SUNDAY   *Moon Age Day 25   Moon Sign Leo*

Make the most of a good period for romance and do what you can to sweep someone completely off their feet. Social relationships should also be very good and will offer you the chance of new friendships, one or two of which might endure for a very long time. This is not to suggest that you ignore old friends, all of whom remain important.

16 MONDAY   *Moon Age Day 26   Moon Sign Virgo*

Handling a heavy workload won't bother you at all as the week gets started though this situation can change significantly as the days go on so make the most of this positive beginning. Clear the decks for action that comes at the far end of the week but don't plan anything too strenuous if family commitments are looming.

17 TUESDAY   *Moon Age Day 27   Moon Sign Virgo*

You definitely enjoy being busy today and can make the best out of almost any sort of circumstance. Watch out for the odd minor mishap, probably brought about as a result of carelessness exhibited by someone else. Your present quick thinking makes you good to have around in any tight corner.

18 WEDNESDAY   *Moon Age Day 28   Moon Sign Libra*

You work best now when at the centre of lots of activity. The hotter the situation the better you will enjoy it and the cut and thrust of life is what keeps you really busy whilst the lunar high is around. Most important of all at present is your ability to get through or around problems that once seemed impossible to solve.

19 THURSDAY   *Moon Age Day 29   Moon Sign Libra*

This is the time to push boundaries and to try things out before you decide you are not equal to the task. You can achieve victories now that would have seemed absolutely impossible just a short while ago and won't be at all fazed by any sort of opposition. Libra is unusually fearless at the moment.

20 FRIDAY
Moon Age Day 0   Moon Sign Libra

The practical world is still doing you the odd favour, allowing you to make gains, particularly in a financial sense. Rules and regulations are not too difficult to follow now and you find yourself well able to conform when it is necessary. Help a friend with a problem and also be supportive of family members.

21 SATURDAY
Moon Age Day 1   Moon Sign Scorpio

It seems that love is mainly where your interests are centred on this October Saturday. You relish the company of someone who cares about you deeply and will do almost anything in return. In more casual attachments, you may be rather confused by the attitude of people who seem self-destructive and who won't take advice.

22 SUNDAY
Moon Age Day 2   Moon Sign Scorpio

You can probably expect a great deal of positive attention coming your way around this time. This will happen in both a personal and in a more general sense. Popularity is everything to you now and you won't hold back in terms of the love you offer in return. Almost anyone can feel your warmth during this most fascinating period.

23 MONDAY
Moon Age Day 3   Moon Sign Sagittarius

It won't be difficult for you to work with people in authority at the moment. You are compliant and more than willing to co-operate, just as long as you consider that the suggestions being made are sensible. There could be some irritations about but these are most likely caused by determination on your part that cannot be utilised yet.

24 TUESDAY
Moon Age Day 4   Moon Sign Sagittarius

This is likely to be a very busy day, even if you are not committed to working. There are gains to be made in your financial dealings and you will probably also be more in tune with family members who have caused you one or two problems recently. Don't wait to be asked in any situation that appeals to you but go for it.

25 WEDNESDAY *Moon Age Day 5 Moon Sign Sagittarius*

You get even more from being on the go today. The Moon is in a good position for you and should prove to be especially helpful when it comes to expressing your emotions. This would be an excellent time for a heart-to-heart with your partner and you are in a good position to think up the sort of compliments that make a difference.

26 THURSDAY *Moon Age Day 6 Moon Sign Capricorn*

As far as your career is concerned you are now likely to go it alone to a greater extent than would normally be the case. This is either because you can't find the advice you need or else because colleagues are not proving quite as reliable as you would wish. Even Libra can be very single-minded and this is certainly the case around now.

27 FRIDAY *Moon Age Day 7 Moon Sign Capricorn*

This is a day when you will be quite happy to be noticed – in fact you are setting your stall out specifically to make sure that you are. You will want to look your best and to attract the sort of people you find alluring and fascinating. Libra is actually quite sexy under present trends and of your attraction to others there will be no doubt.

28 SATURDAY *Moon Age Day 8 Moon Sign Aquarius*

Progress in your daily life is no more than steady today but that doesn't mean you fail to make any headway at all. Prior planning is important, together with getting little details sorted out that will make your path easier in a day or two. However, you will have to be patient as far as practical movement is concerned.

29 SUNDAY *Moon Age Day 9 Moon Sign Aquarius*

Today should be quite light-hearted and demands a very gentle touch. Any tendency to get too serious about anything won't meet with a good response from others, so show just how humorous and jolly you are capable of being. This is especially necessary in personal attachments and with regard to romance.

30 MONDAY

Moon Age Day 10   Moon Sign Pisces

This will be one of the best days of the week for busy preparations and for making sure that everything you need is in place for your plans to mature later. If you are working on several different fronts at the same time you could find yourself running out of steam if you also go for a very hectic social time this evening.

31 TUESDAY

Moon Age Day 11   Moon Sign Pisces

You may have your work cut out today in solving problems that are caused, in the main, by colleagues or even friends. Most situations will be quite easy to deal with and you tend to approach life with a very good attitude. If anyone is the joker in the pack around this time it is almost certain to be you.

1 WEDNESDAY   *Moon Age Day 12   Moon Sign Pisces*

It's already the first day of November and you will probably be left wondering where much of the year has actually gone. If you look back though, you should see just how far you have come in many respects and you are still planning events and gatherings that will fall within this year. Try to remain as optimistic as possible today.

2 THURSDAY   *Moon Age Day 13   Moon Sign Aries*

The arrival of the lunar low is inclined to put the brakes on as far as some of your more practical efforts are concerned and you could quite easily discover that a slower and steadier approach is called for. People in the know are in a good position to offer you some sound advice and right now you have sufficient time to listen to them.

3 FRIDAY   *Moon Age Day 14   Moon Sign Aries*

Life can seem fairly demanding, whilst at the same time failing to offer you quite the same incentives you have come to expect of late. Everything you get seems to come hard but at least you are applying yourself and won't be easily beaten. In some situations it might be that you are trying just a little too hard.

4 SATURDAY   *Moon Age Day 15   Moon Sign Taurus*

There is a slightly testing phase on the way for your partnerships, whether these are of a personal or a professional sort. It looks as though you are inclined to go solo for the moment and that might be part of what is causing the potential problems. This is out of character because you are usually so good at sharing.

5 SUNDAY   *Moon Age Day 16   Moon Sign Taurus*

You will benefit greatly today from getting together with others and discussing almost anything under the sun. Some of the best answers you find at the moment can come as a result of these discussions and since you are in a very 'think tank' mentality, the more people you draw into your circle, the better the results should be.

6 MONDAY   *Moon Age Day 17   Moon Sign Gemini*

Partnerships are likely to take up a great deal of your time as you work hard to bring someone round to a point of view that seems quite self-evident to you. No matter how hard you try, you may have difficulty persuading people to follow your lead and if this is the case you will have to work especially hard to find a compromise.

7 TUESDAY   *Moon Age Day 18   Moon Sign Gemini*

The big lesson to learn today is that you cannot and should not exert a possessive influence on those close to you. It is not the right way forward to try to make them change to suit your needs and in any case you will be more likely to have a positive influence on them if you allow them to decide for themselves.

8 WEDNESDAY   *Moon Age Day 19   Moon Sign Cancer*

A period of some mental pressure comes along, but probably only because you have so many potential choices to make. Try not to dwell too much on specific issues and allow your intuition to be at least part of your guide. This is because your usual common sense might not be enough to get you the answers you need.

9 THURSDAY   *Moon Age Day 20   Moon Sign Cancer*

Good communications with relatives and with your partner will be needed today if you are to solve a slight problem or series of problems that will become obvious at home. There is a great deal to be said at the moment for sticking with a few routines and also for allowing others to take some of the strain.

10 FRIDAY   *Moon Age Day 21   Moon Sign Leo*

This might not be the most romantic period of the month but it does offer certain benefits that have a bearing on personal attachments. You are a good talker and also a great listener around this time. Because you are so attentive people who tend to have kept things somewhat hidden for a while should now open up.

11 SATURDAY   *Moon Age Day 22   Moon Sign Leo*

Paradoxically for those of you who do not work at the weekend, today offers some of the very best professional prospects of the week. You are quite decisive now and won't leave anything to chance. Domestic prospects are very slightly less rosy, perhaps because those around you are tetchy or inclined to be over-critical about something.

12 SUNDAY   *Moon Age Day 23   Moon Sign Virgo*

This is a time during which you can capitalise on your ability to do something novel or different. Getting out to places of culture and learning something on the way could prove to be very important to Libra under present trends. What's more, you are inspiring others with your refreshing attitudes and your deep knowledge.

13 MONDAY   *Moon Age Day 24   Moon Sign Virgo*

Expect a fairly unsettled period early in the week. People you meet in a professional or social sense don't seem to be making much sense and you will constantly have to make allowances for them. Nothing feels reliable to you and the only time things go the way you would expect is when you attend to them yourself.

14 TUESDAY   *Moon Age Day 25   Moon Sign Libra*

Today have an awareness of your individuality and won't be at all inclined to stay in the background. Wherever there is action, that is where you will choose to be because Libra is now about as dynamic and driven as it is possible for the zodiac sign to be. It should be relatively easy to get your own way.

15 WEDNESDAY   *Moon Age Day 26   Moon Sign Libra*

You now have quite an unusual response to what life offers you, with the result that you are living your life in a fairly unique way. The attraction you have for others isn't at all in doubt and you can turn heads wherever you go. This period isn't all about work because from a social point of view you can sizzle.

16 THURSDAY   *Moon Age Day 27   Moon Sign Libra*

Your personal life is emphasised now and you will probably be concentrating on those issues that are going to make you feel happier and more contented in the weeks and months ahead. Family discussions could be on the cards and there are positive gains to be made from knowing how others feel.

17 FRIDAY   *Moon Age Day 28   Moon Sign Scorpio*

Something about today might make you feel let down. If this is the case you can be sure that the root of this feeling is mental and emotional because there probably will not be anything going wrong in a practical sense. It's up to you to keep pushing forward and to ignore the fact that you may be feeling slightly down.

18 SATURDAY   *Moon Age Day 0   Moon Sign Scorpio*

This will be a time of great insight, when your intuitive nature works overtime. When it comes to assessing others you will now be second to none and you won't easily be fooled, either in a practical or a personal sense. There may be significant room for compromise regarding a disagreement somewhere in the family.

19 SUNDAY   *Moon Age Day 1   Moon Sign Sagittarius*

Those you meet socially will stimulate your own thinking and may bring you to alternative strategies and ingenious ideas that were not in place only a day or two ago. Mentally speaking you will be as bright as a button and it would take someone extremely clever to get one over on you. Your cognitive skills are now excellent.

20 MONDAY   *Moon Age Day 2   Moon Sign Sagittarius*

This is a time of excitement and change – a period when you can't necessarily wait for others to keep up and when you will be very keen to follow the dictates of your own will. Of course there are occasions when you can't ignore the needs of those around you but with your present ingenuity you can somehow incorporate them.

21 TUESDAY   *Moon Age Day 3   Moon Sign Sagittarius*

You like to be noticed and will probably be actively doing things to make sure that you are not overlooked. When it comes to getting what you want in a professional sense, commitment and intent are both extremely important at the moment. You seem to have a knowing knack of being in the right place at the right time.

22 WEDNESDAY   *Moon Age Day 4   Moon Sign Capricorn*

Life is not a rehearsal, as you are about to discover. Instead of waiting around to see what might happen, today is a time to get busy and to make things mature in the way you would wish. There is no end to your own power under present trends but it all depends on your own attitude and your willingness to become involved.

23 THURSDAY   *Moon Age Day 5   Moon Sign Capricorn*

Right at this moment in time you want to be number one. Since you rarely have a selfish bone in your body there is nothing at all wrong with being self-centred once in a while. What's more, you should discover that those who care about you the most will be anxious to let you have your own way. Even some strangers might join in.

24 FRIDAY   *Moon Age Day 6   Moon Sign Aquarius*

You should now be on a winning streak in a professional sense and it looks as though you will be readily acting upon new opportunities that come your way. This part of November could turn out to be quite exciting and to offer possibilities that would have seemed out of the question even a few short months ago.

25 SATURDAY   *Moon Age Day 7   Moon Sign Aquarius*

You continue to seek adventure, though now you tend to do so through romance. If you have more than one admirer at the moment you might be busy doing some sort of balancing act! Even Librans who feel themselves to be settled in a romantic sense could find the flame of love burning much brighter.

26 SUNDAY   *Moon Age Day 8   Moon Sign Aquarius*

Don't be distracted by the demands made upon you by friends and family members. Although you may have time to think about domestic issues on a Sunday, at the same time there is plenty of potential excitement about too. It might be necessary to split your day but avoid giving yourself entirely to anything tedious or demanding.

27 MONDAY   *Moon Age Day 9   Moon Sign Pisces*

Leave behind anything that is inclined to drag you down. This might seem the worst time of the year for a spring clean in the general sense of the expression but as far as your mind goes, this is the best period of all. A new year is not that far away and you don't want to carry too much surplus baggage on into December.

28 TUESDAY   *Moon Age Day 10   Moon Sign Pisces*

Powerful emotions are stirred up in your mind and it is towards home and family that most of your thinking is directed. Beware of frayed tempers and don't put yourself in a position where others will accuse you of being bossy. Beware, also, a couple of trends that mean a little temper is in evidence when you are at home.

29 WEDNESDAY   *Moon Age Day 11   Moon Sign Aries*

This may not be the luckiest day of the month, especially in any practical sense. You have the lunar low to cope with and this can take the wind out of your sails in a number of different ways. Rely on what others can do for you and take some rest. You will be back up to speed before you know it but rushing today won't help.

30 THURSDAY   *Moon Age Day 12   Moon Sign Aries*

This is another day that more or less demands you take things at a calmer pace and don't get involved in issues that will sap your energy and resolve. You will tire easily at the moment, which is why you need to watch and wait. By tomorrow things should be back to normal, but for the moment simply relax.

December 2017

1 FRIDAY
Moon Age Day 13   Moon Sign Taurus

It looks as though you will have your detective hat on today. Just about everything interests you but what stands out is your present rampant curiosity. When it comes to working out why things happen in the way they do you will leave no stone unturned – and you are likely to have a good time on the way.

2 SATURDAY
Moon Age Day 14   Moon Sign Taurus

For a number of planetary reasons your interests now tend to turn towards mental and philosophical considerations. Some Librans will even by gaining a new spiritual dimension to their lives or else embarking on some sort of health kick that brings intellectual depth as well as stronger muscles. Don't push yourself too hard.

3 SUNDAY
☿ *Moon Age Day 15   Moon Sign Gemini*

A new phase is underway and it is one that may challenge you to renew and revitalise certain aspects of your life that have become dull or unworkable. Of necessity this means leaving something behind and that isn't necessarily easy for Libra. Excess baggage isn't important though and it is getting in your way.

4 MONDAY
☿ *Moon Age Day 16   Moon Sign Gemini*

Self-criticism at the start of this working week can stem from too great an expectation of yourself and your recent efforts. A more modest approach to situations seems to be called for, together with a greater ability to relax into life. The more content you make yourself, the better most aspects of your life will seem to be.

5 TUESDAY ☿ *Moon Age Day 17 Moon Sign Cancer*

You may discover today how important it is to plan your next strategy because certain situations will unravel like a ball of wool if you trust to luck. This need not be a problem because Libra is now about as organised as any zodiac sign can be. Unforced errors are not very likely but concentration is still necessary.

6 WEDNESDAY ☿ *Moon Age Day 18 Moon Sign Cancer*

You can get what you want today with the aid of a little persuasion and you won't easily be put off by the slightly negative attitudes of people with whom you have to deal. Avoid getting involved in arguments of any sort but particularly those that you know instinctively are going to lead you nowhere at all.

7 THURSDAY ☿ *Moon Age Day 19 Moon Sign Leo*

The way ahead now looks fairly clear, though you view it from a sort of platform and won't be putting in too much in the way of direct physical effort for the moment. For some days now you should have been ridding yourself of baggage that you don't want to carry forward into the coming year. Expect some new incentives to come along, too.

8 FRIDAY ☿ *Moon Age Day 20 Moon Sign Leo*

It would be a great advantage today to continue your general efforts to get on well – but whilst also learning the value of relaxation. The situation is helped if you tackle one task at a time and don't crowd yourself with tasks that aren't at all necessary. You can also get on better if you learn to delegate.

9 SATURDAY ☿ *Moon Age Day 21 Moon Sign Virgo*

You might now have to rethink a pet project very carefully, especially if it is becoming obvious to you that something isn't working in the way you had hoped. There is no point at all in ploughing on regardless, when a slight alteration to the way you behave can make all the difference.

10 SUNDAY ☿ *Moon Age Day 22   Moon Sign Virgo*

Your love of travel is likely to show itself and you will soon feel dull and disinterested if you don't get some change into almost every aspect of your life. What started out as a little restlessness has now become something much more. Avoid unnecessary routines and opt for as many diversions as you can find.

11 MONDAY ☿ *Moon Age Day 23   Moon Sign Virgo*

You may feel compelled to move forward, probably at work, even if other people seem to be dragging their feet. It seems as if there is no stopping you at the moment and you rise to challenges in a moment. At home you may decide to make alterations to décor or change things round in some way, maybe ahead of Christmas.

12 TUESDAY ☿ *Moon Age Day 24   Moon Sign Libra*

Your sense of timing is impeccable and you will be anxious to make headway in practical matters. You should now be less geared towards negative thoughts and on the contrary your mind can concentrate on very positive issues to do with career and money. There is a stronger element of good luck attending your actions.

13 WEDNESDAY ☿ *Moon Age Day 25   Moon Sign Libra*

Your mind is working overtime and you have sufficient energy at the moment for your body to keep up. Your health seems to be in good shape and if there have been any issues in that direction recently, these could now be resolved. All things considered, this should be the most positive time of the month for you.

14 THURSDAY ☿ *Moon Age Day 26   Moon Sign Scorpio*

Avoid conflicts in your love life by refusing to get involved in pointless discussions or even arguments. It isn't you who is being reactive but rather those around you, but you could so easily be drawn into rows. For most of the time you are as calm and easy-going as anything but you can display a stubborn streak right now.

15 FRIDAY   ☿ *Moon Age Day 27   Moon Sign Scorpio*

Today could be especially good for all business matters, since you display a healthy mix of optimism and caution. This is Libra at its best and it stands you in good stead when it comes to making money. Planning projects should be easy and you have such a good understanding with colleagues at present they should follow your lead.

16 SATURDAY   ☿ *Moon Age Day 28   Moon Sign Scorpio*

Romance could bring a little tension on this particular Saturday and you will need to make sure you don't take offence over something that isn't really important. There are challenges to be faced if you are at work, though these tend to be quite positive in nature. It's important for the moment not to react too harshly to nothing in particular.

17 SUNDAY   ☿ *Moon Age Day 29   Moon Sign Sagittarius*

Your interest in travel, which has been increasing steadily throughout this month, is now getting quite intense. You actively need fresh fields and pastures new, even though those around you might have very different ideas. Short trips will do the trick for a while but what you really want is a long and luxurious holiday. Fat chance!

18 MONDAY   ☿ *Moon Age Day 0   Moon Sign Sagittarius*

A little soul searching may be necessary in order for you to come to terms with certain aspects of your life as they appear now. In your anxiety to make almost everything different there is a very real chance you might throw out the baby with the bathwater. You might have to put on the brakes a little after making conscious decisions.

19 TUESDAY   ☿ *Moon Age Day 1   Moon Sign Capricorn*

A sense of co-operation that probably did not exist a few days ago now makes itself felt. You have an upbeat emotional outlook and will be far less likely to get involved in disputes that lead to arguments. The Moon is in a useful position for you at the moment and that turns out to be especially good when dealing with your family.

20 WEDNESDAY ☿ *Moon Age Day 2   Moon Sign Capricorn*

A personal issue may show the extent to which you have your work cut out. This can be quite a reactive sort of day but you should still make progress and enjoy yourself if you approach matters in the right way. Stop and think before you make momentous decisions and do your best to avoid cluttering up your life with pointless items.

21 THURSDAY ☿ *Moon Age Day 3   Moon Sign Capricorn*

You have a strong drive to make a good impression all round. If you are meeting new people, which is quite likely, you will want to put in the extra effort to make the most of what could turn out to be deep friendships. Don't get too involved in the personal problems of a friend. Give advice but stay away from intrigue.

22 FRIDAY ☿ *Moon Age Day 4   Moon Sign Aquarius*

There is some strong support to be had today, particularly at work. It looks as though you will be busy but that isn't too surprising with Christmas only a few days away. Take some time out to remember all those people for whom you haven't bought presents and do something about it today.

23 SATURDAY *Moon Age Day 5   Moon Sign Aquarius*

You can make some progress at work, that is if you happen to work at the weekend, but otherwise this should be a fairly steady sort of day. The chances are that you will be preparing yourself for the upcoming festivities and you can enjoy a fairly settled family time if you put your mind to it. There is still some restlessness about.

24 SUNDAY *Moon Age Day 6   Moon Sign Pisces*

Today bring a steady start but with a rapid improvement as the day moves on. Christmas Eve should find you anxious to move about freely, less held back by details and more inclined to get out there and have a good time. Last minute details can be sorted out and you have a great ability to create fun at the drop of a hat.

25 MONDAY
Moon Age Day 7   Moon Sign Pisces

Travel is positively highlighted for Christmas Day, so maybe at least part of the day will be spent somewhere other than in your own home. Whether this proves to be the case or not you are likely to be very cheerful and quite imaginative. Your present attitude is just right for having fun yourself and promoting it for others.

26 TUESDAY
Moon Age Day 8   Moon Sign Pisces

When you are involved in discussions today you could find that the people around you are proving to be more argumentative than you may have expected. Keep your patience and to explain yourself as fully as you can. If things still don't go the way you want you must either compromise or else do your own thing.

27 WEDNESDAY
Moon Age Day 9   Moon Sign Aries

There is every reason to feel left behind today as you enter the lunar low for December. It might be slightly trying but at least you will get this less-than-favourable phase out of the way before New Year arrives. Stand and stare for a while, whilst you let other people do some jobs for you. This isn't selfish – it's sensible.

28 THURSDAY
Moon Age Day 10   Moon Sign Aries

Expect anything but smooth progress, even though the things that go wrong are not really important. Frustrations may be evident and you should take special care if you have to start anything new at this time. Seek expert advice from people who know what they are talking about and avoid all cowboys!

29 FRIDAY
Moon Age Day 11   Moon Sign Taurus

Be open to new input today and allow yourself the right to change your mind if you know instinctively it is necessary to do so. This might involve you in some fairly deep discussions in order to explain yourself but you have a silver tongue at the moment and won't have any trouble getting others to agree with you.

30 SATURDAY   *Moon Age Day 12   Moon Sign Taurus*

Romantic issues may throw up the odd challenge so pay attention in order to make certain you are saying and doing the right things. It might seem as if there are tests around now, custom-made to make sure that you are thinking and acting in the right way. Some new hobby or pastime could be on the cards.

31 SUNDAY   *Moon Age Day 13   Moon Sign Gemini*

You are certainly not a shrinking violet as the year draws towards its close. You intend to be fully in the social and personal spotlight and that is where you will undoubtedly feel most comfortable at the moment. Compliments come from many different directions – though you might be too busy to notice them.

LIBRA:
2018 DIARY PAGES

LIBRA:
YOUR YEAR IN BRIEF

It is a fact that Libra is a zodiac sign that prefers to be on the go so you will be happy to learn that this is possible almost from the very start of the year. Get yourself into the right position to make advancements at work and do all you can to elevate yourself in the minds of bosses and superiors. These trends, though altering from day to day, perpetuate throughout most of January and February bringing a chance for you to shine.

It is towards personal associations that your mind is apt to turn at the beginning of the spring. Don't be too quick to let go of some important relationships and try to spend time with those who know you the best. Avoid financial speculation during March and April, although prepare for some significant non-monetary successes. Love shines out late in April.

With the arrival of early summer, May and June find you curious about the way the world works and anxious to do all you can to show your positive side to everyone you meet. Your desire to make others realise how good life can be is well marked and the joy you bring to situations is clear. Not everyone welcomes your help at present but most people will be glad to have you around and will rely on your advice.

The high summer looks as though it will be an excellent time for you and offers much of what you could desire in terms of movement and a little more excitement entering your life. At the same time July and August find you in a very family-motivated frame of mind and very capable of relaxation. Get successful people at work on side and follow their lead as much as you can.

September and October are likely to be months filled with enterprise and possibility. Not everything you want is likely to come your way – or at least this might appear to be the case at first. In the main you deal with all eventualities in your usual, efficient way and you have a distinct advantage at this time when it comes to working out what people around you are thinking. Libra is especially intuitive at this time.

The last two months of the year offer diversions and very strong social inclinations on your part. There is nothing strange about this for Libra but you are really shining during November and December and so will almost certainly be noticed. Look out for a possible change within your career or perhaps a new job altogether. Make the most of the festive season when it comes along and show just how ingenious and inspiring you can be. The end of the year should be amazing.

January 2018

1 MONDAY
Moon Age Day 14   Moon Sign Gemini

Partnerships function best when you avoid extremes of any kind, either in attitude or action. Stay middle of the road in your plans and co-operate as much as possible with your partner. This is just as important in a business partnership as it is in a romantic one. This is no time to be going off at a Libran tangent.

2 TUESDAY
Moon Age Day 15   Moon Sign Cancer

With a deep desire to succeed at the moment, especially where work is concerned, what you get out of life is directly proportional to the amount of effort you put in. Your confidence remains essentially high when you are taking on challenges you have either chosen yourself or ones you understand.

3 WEDNESDAY
Moon Age Day 16   Moon Sign Cancer

Being considerate of others does not necessarily mean having to compromise all the time. You can follow your own thoughts and let those around you know the way you are thinking, whether or not they choose to follow suit. In the end most of your present hunches should turn out to be more or less correct.

4 THURSDAY
Moon Age Day 17   Moon Sign Leo

Your competitive nature is easily stimulated now and you need to get your own way in most situations. Whether this turns out to be possible remains to be seen but you might get slightly cranky if you sense your will is being blocked. At home you should find relationships to be generally harmonious.

5 FRIDAY
Moon Age Day 18   Moon Sign Leo

In close partnerships you may lack a certain tolerance for the beliefs of others, which is most unlike you. This is a very short trend and is brought about by the position of the Moon. Don't take any prohibitive actions today and avoid reacting to things that would normally go over your head. Better to spend time alone than to argue.

6 SATURDAY
Moon Age Day 19   Moon Sign Virgo

You should be able to score some significant successes today and you won't be too put out if you have to alter your ideas at a moment's notice. You are now beginning to take life very much more in your stride and as a result you show yourself to the world much more as a typical Air sign individual should.

7 SUNDAY
Moon Age Day 20   Moon Sign Virgo

You can now afford to be bold and ambitious, something that hasn't really been the case too much during the first week of January. It could feel now as if life has been ticking over and then suddenly you find you are in gear. You are likely to be at your most effective when you are amongst people who stimulate your imagination.

8 MONDAY
Moon Age Day 21   Moon Sign Libra

Today should be extremely progressive and responds well to movement and activity as far as you are concerned. Do your best to put yourself about in a social sense and don't be at all surprised if you discover you are flavour of the month. When it comes to romance you will prove just how sexy you can be.

9 TUESDAY
Moon Age Day 22   Moon Sign Libra

As you really get going into the working week the Moon remains in Libra, which means you will be determined and dynamic. This is a time when extra responsibility may come your way but this is likely to be of a sort that you accept without question. Get to know people who have been strangers up to now because new friends are possible.

10 WEDNESDAY   *Moon Age Day 23   Moon Sign Scorpio*

Feelings now run close to the surface in a personal sense and you can't really avoid showing others what you feel about them. Generally, you are easy to deal with and remain popular with colleagues and friends alike. However, there may be one specific person that you can't get on with at any price.

11 THURSDAY   *Moon Age Day 24   Moon Sign Scorpio*

Though you remain ready for action, especially at work, don't expect absolutely everything to go your way. You may require some help from others in a practical sense and you might find that things go more smoothly when you co-operating with colleagues. In particular, recognise that professional advice is sometimes essential.

12 FRIDAY   *Moon Age Day 25   Moon Sign Scorpio*

Certain situations are unlikely to work in the way you might have expected. Potential pitfalls are evident and it is difficult to know exactly how to proceed. None of this turns out to be especially important because problems brought by the lunar aspects are often insubstantial. Watch and wait until tomorrow.

13 SATURDAY   *Moon Age Day 26   Moon Sign Sagittarius*

You are likely to enjoy indulging your imagination today – and probably for some days to come. Working out how things might happen 'if' can be fun, even if you never actually get the chance to try. None of this will prevent your practical side from taking over when there are real jobs to be done.

14 SUNDAY   *Moon Age Day 27   Moon Sign Sagittarius*

Pay attention when it comes to major negotiations of just about any sort. Don't take anything for granted and check and re-check all appointments and arrangements to avoid complications later. Newer and better financial opportunities are on the way and might begin to show themselves at any time.

15 MONDAY   *Moon Age Day 28   Moon Sign Capricorn*

You express yourself with grace and style during the course of today, especially this evening. Everything in your world is likely to be harmonious and if it isn't, you will be doing your best to make it so. Positive feelings abound and you know how to get others to do your bidding under almost any circumstance.

16 TUESDAY   *Moon Age Day 0   Moon Sign Capricorn*

Because you are slightly more confused and less focused than usual, you may have to work that much harder in order to get things running the way you want. Don't worry if you don't seem to be getting ahead very much in a practical sense because it's plain that as far as your personal life is concerned, everything is much more settled.

17 WEDNESDAY   *Moon Age Day 1   Moon Sign Capricorn*

There may be some preoccupation with past matters, which might be a pity when so much is going on around you right now, but in a general sense, things continue to go more or less your way. As far as making important decisions is concerned, there are a number of reasons why you should probably leave them until tomorrow.

18 THURSDAY   *Moon Age Day 2   Moon Sign Aquarius*

Focus your sights on friendships, which are likely to be working out rather well for you at this time. You could be making a pal of someone you didn't get on with in the past, or else finding new attachments that come like a bolt from the blue. You can meet people almost anywhere today – and probably will.

19 FRIDAY   *Moon Age Day 3   Moon Sign Aquarius*

Travel and communication seem to be the answers to any problem that surrounds you right now. The more you are flexible and willing to fall in line with good ideas that come from other directions, the better the day is likely to be. You certainly won't be afraid to work hard now if you know it will benefit you.

20 SATURDAY
Moon Age Day 4   Moon Sign Pisces

This is a very favourable period for getting along with other people. 'The more the merrier' seems to be your adage for the next couple of days and you know very well how to make people feel comfortable. As a result you can get any assistance you need quite easily and won't be put off by anyone less cheerful.

21 SUNDAY
Moon Age Day 5   Moon Sign Pisces

Right now new friendships could be a source of great delight and pleasure to you. You should also be feeling quite fulfilled as a result of what others are saying and doing. It may almost seem as if you have to do little or nothing in order to get those around you to do what you think is best. Your intuition remains very strong.

22 MONDAY
Moon Age Day 6   Moon Sign Pisces

Take care not to misconstrue what other people are saying under present trends. If you are not certain, ask again, and again if necessary. Once you are in possession of the facts you will know how to proceed and tend to do so with great certainty and speed. You may have quite a lot on your plate for the moment.

23 TUESDAY
Moon Age Day 7   Moon Sign Aries

Today's challenges come through personal relationships and the way you approach all sorts of associations with other people. Not everyone seems to be on your side at the moment and that means you will have to be more accommodating than ever or risk an argument. The best course of action is just to carry on in your own sweet way.

24 WEDNESDAY
Moon Age Day 8   Moon Sign Aries

Keep a lid on some of your emotions because you won't gain anything today by being absolutely truthful about the way you feel. In any case your mood is changing all the time at the moment, making this a bad time for burning any bridges. Things are likely to be sluggish whilst the lunar low is around.

25 THURSDAY   *Moon Age Day 9   Moon Sign Taurus*

When given the chance to learn something new you are likely to grab it with both hands. This is the most positive side of Libra shining out and it is a situation that continues, on and off, for the next month at least. Your cheerfulness and kindliness can be the reason that others experience delight in their own lives.

26 FRIDAY   *Moon Age Day 10   Moon Sign Taurus*

This is likely to be a very progressive phase in terms of your career and a time during which you are thinking about all those changes you want to make. You instinctively know how things could be better all-round. Even if some people disagree or hold back, you will still be racing on towards your objectives.

27 SATURDAY   *Moon Age Day 11   Moon Sign Gemini*

Friendships seem to be source of great joy and amusement this weekend. Although you will be quite committed to home and family in some respects, it's clear that you need to have your pals surrounding you at some stage. You might be able to mix the two, by inviting people round and spending some time with them at home.

28 SUNDAY   *Moon Age Day 12   Moon Sign Gemini*

A phase is now on the way during which favourable highlights fall on group activities and upon the relationships you have with people in the outside world. This does not mean you will be ignoring your nearest and dearest, though there is a slight possibility that this could be the case today. Everything comes more into focus later.

29 MONDAY   *Moon Age Day 13   Moon Sign Cancer*

This is a time for getting to grips with anything you feel is holding you back. Take control of your own forces and don't be put off just because some other people think your ideas don't have merit. If you persevere you will prove something to yourself and to them. Friendship is especially important under present trends.

30 TUESDAY   *Moon Age Day 14   Moon Sign Cancer*

Future prospects look generally good and you seem to have what it takes to make others sit up and take notice of you. All major dreams and schemes have a place today and although you can't do everything as quickly as you might wish, you will get there in the end. In social settings you can shine like a star.

31 WEDNESDAY   *Moon Age Day 15   Moon Sign Leo*

You would do very well to avoid confrontations of almost any sort today. You are still friendly and approachable but unfortunately not everyone feels quite the same way. There is also a possibility that you will underestimate certain situations. You can't afford to gloss over anything and it is important that you stay focused.

♎ February 2018

1 THURSDAY
Moon Age Day 16   Moon Sign Leo

This might prove to be a key moment as far as progress of a practical sort is concerned. Some of the blockages that were evident during January are now disappearing altogether and you should find that you move forward very positively as a result. People should recognise you are a winner and want to be part of your game.

2 FRIDAY
Moon Age Day 17   Moon Sign Virgo

Planetary trends now put you on a winning streak as far as love is concerned and you are extremely popular when mixing with people you know and also those you do not. Conversation comes as easy to you as breathing and you are now able to talk freely to anyone – and on a host of different topics.

3 SATURDAY
Moon Age Day 18   Moon Sign Virgo

Untypically it is possible you will be in an argumentative mood with others today, though of course you will tell yourself it is they who are behaving unreasonably. Nevertheless it takes two to tango and if you refuse to become involved arguments cannot take place. Later in the day there are likely to be some unexpected social invitations.

4 SUNDAY
Moon Age Day 19   Moon Sign Libra

Getting your own way with others is now not at all difficult. You continue to take a few chances, though these are of a calculated sort because you are also quite careful under present planetary trends. Wherever you look today there is likely to be scope for interest and advancement. Your cheerful nature is a joy to behold.

5 MONDAY   *Moon Age Day 20   Moon Sign Libra*

Your ability to communicate with others is always good but at the moment it should be positively legendary. It doesn't matter what sort of people you are associating with, what does matter is that you can easily adapt your own nature to suit theirs. You might decide that this particular Monday would be a good time to take a trip.

6 TUESDAY   *Moon Age Day 21   Moon Sign Libra*

The pace of your social life is now inclined to quicken and you are waking up more and more to the opportunities that February is bringing. Today's events are likely to be mentally stimulating and you are filled with a sense of anticipation regarding new plans. Family members want to have you around today and you may comply.

7 WEDNESDAY   *Moon Age Day 22   Moon Sign Scorpio*

The time is right to follow your heart, especially as far as relationships are concerned. You are self-motivating at the moment and have tremendous inner strength, which is why you can achieve almost anything you set out to do. At work it is possible that rules and regulations might get in the way but there are ways round them.

8 THURSDAY   *Moon Age Day 23   Moon Sign Scorpio*

One-to-one relationships might seem slightly downbeat today and you will need to be fairly tactful and understanding if you are to retain the closeness that you cherish. Don't worry, because it is impossible for people to see eye-to-eye all the time and there may be hidden stresses that you don't fully appreciate.

9 FRIDAY   *Moon Age Day 24   Moon Sign Sagittarius*

Though finances should be looking good you would be wise to show a degree of common sense when it comes to buying luxury items right now. If you choose to look around instead of opting for the first thing you see, you could get an undoubted bargain. At work you tend to be very inventive and quite successful around now.

10 SATURDAY   *Moon Age Day 25   Moon Sign Sagittarius*

You can be very warm and supportive to your friends and quite approachable to strangers too. There is a private side to your personality that is not difficult to spot and this is emphasised by present planetary trends. This may seem slightly at odds with the more gregarious side of your nature that is also strong now.

11 SUNDAY   *Moon Age Day 26   Moon Sign Sagittarius*

Build upon recent successes and look after your finances carefully around now. Personal security probably matters a great deal to you at this time and you especially concerned about your long-term financial prospects. Although you were willing to take a few little chances early in the month you are far less likely to be doing so today.

12 MONDAY   *Moon Age Day 27   Moon Sign Capricorn*

Your partner may be on a short fuse today so take care to avoid causing upsets by saying or doing the wrong thing. Let them take the lead and be a follower for a few hours. At least that way you can't get things wrong. Outside of personal attachments you will still be in command of most situations.

13 TUESDAY   *Moon Age Day 28   Moon Sign Capricorn*

This may be one of the better days of the year so far during which you can experience a sense of personal freedom. Nothing much has changed apart from your attitude but that's what really matters to a Libran. If you believe that something is possible, the chances are it will be so. Friends should be accommodating.

14 WEDNESDAY   *Moon Age Day 29   Moon Sign Aquarius*

Daily issues should work out more or less the way you want, though not without a few setbacks. Of course you are quite dynamic at the moment and in some respects you might be moving too quickly. There are moments today when it would be sensible to stop and stare for a while. If you act in haste you may regret it later.

15 THURSDAY *Moon Age Day 0   Moon Sign Aquarius*

Now you have a heartfelt approach to others and the way you treat them is an indication of the sort of person you are. Nothing seems to be too much trouble and you will be happy to put yourself out for a good cause. In company you are good to have around and can inspire people on to greater things.

16 FRIDAY *Moon Age Day 1   Moon Sign Aquarius*

This is a time when being on the move is not only fairly essential but also quite enjoyable. You know what you want from life and will be moving as fast as you can to get it. Some people around you will be slowed down by the time of year and the wintry weather but that doesn't apply to you too much.

17 SATURDAY *Moon Age Day 2   Moon Sign Pisces*

There could be some slight relationship difficulties today and these come about partly because you are nowhere near as understanding and easy-going as would normally be the case. You might be able to see some of your destinations in life, but that doesn't mean you can get to them as quickly as you wish.

18 SUNDAY *Moon Age Day 3   Moon Sign Pisces*

You may have a lot on your mind and a strong need to communicate right now. In a way it doesn't really matter who you talk to because what is important is that you put your feelings into words. Once you have done so you should feel better and some of the complications in your mind should begin to clear.

19 MONDAY *Moon Age Day 4   Moon Sign Aries*

You have now entered a planetary lull and the only way to deal with it is to admit that you can't keep moving forward at your accustomed speed. It won't do you any harm to sit back and watch the flowers grow for a while – if you can find any at this time of year! Give yourself some valuable thinking time.

20 TUESDAY   *Moon Age Day 5   Moon Sign Aries*

The time is now right to pursue money matters but to do so from the comfort of your own favourite chair. You will be less inclined to push yourself forward during today, but by tomorrow more powerful trends take over again and the lunar low will be out of the way. You may not physically wander far but your mind can take fantastic journeys.

21 WEDNESDAY   *Moon Age Day 6   Moon Sign Taurus*

Don't hang back when it comes to important initiatives, even though in some senses you still need to watch and wait. This is a bit of a conundrum. If you have to move forward, how can you also stand and think? It's a problem you can solve by looking at aspects of your life in an entirely different way.

22 THURSDAY   *Moon Age Day 7   Moon Sign Taurus*

There could be some setbacks in your love life, but not if you take the time out to really talk to your partner and to come to terms over an issue about which you haven't been able to agree recently. You seem to have some fairly deep matters on your mind and you might think that others won't understand – but in reality they will.

23 FRIDAY   *Moon Age Day 8   Moon Sign Taurus*

Emotional matters could prove to be a test of your strength today and you will have to keep your temper, even when people and circumstances sorely try you. Intense feelings may come to the surface and have to be dealt with. Stick to casual friends and acquaintances if at all possible.

24 SATURDAY   *Moon Age Day 9   Moon Sign Gemini*

A steady financial improvement is now on the cards. Partly this is due to the actions you have been taking for some time, together with a dose of general good luck that surrounds you at this time. With the Sun in its present position you will be spending a good deal of time getting to grips with practical necessities.

25 SUNDAY   *Moon Age Day 10   Moon Sign Gemini*

What a great period this is for friendships. It might be said to have been the case that earlier this month you had difficulty getting truly onside with loved ones, and sometimes even with colleagues. Now you are so adaptable you can see eye-to-eye with almost anyone without compromising your own principles.

26 MONDAY   *Moon Age Day 11   Moon Sign Cancer*

It appears that your skill for attracting new people into your life is very good at this time. Contrary to the opinions of some, you are able to communicate well and may prove this more than one occasion now. There are times later in the day when it ought to be possible to tell your partner how you really feel.

27 TUESDAY   *Moon Age Day 12   Moon Sign Cancer*

You are likely to be very progressive when it comes to practical improvements you want to make around yourself, most likely at home. You will find you have more time to talk to your loved ones and especially to your partner. This means a better and more harmonious set of surroundings and great encouragement coming your way.

28 WEDNESDAY   *Moon Age Day 13   Moon Sign Leo*

A change is as good as a rest to Libra, especially so today. If you get the chance of a journey, grab it with both hands. Your creative potential is strong and you might actually hang around long enough in one place to reveal this to people. Don't stack up too much work now because you need to relax.

March

2018

1 THURSDAY
Moon Age Day 14   Moon Sign Leo

This should prove to be a very rewarding phase in terms of personal relationships. Librans who have been looking for love should keep their eyes wide open because it might be just around the next corner. Do your best to get things in context, especially concerning younger family members and their present behaviour.

2 FRIDAY
Moon Age Day 15   Moon Sign Virgo

Life may be getting rather too serious for your liking and so you will do your best to lighten things as much as possible. Cheer up your friends and motivate them to get on with something new – if only so that they are more fun to have around. By the evening you could be confronting some of your demons.

3 SATURDAY
Moon Age Day 16   Moon Sign Virgo

A total change of scenery would suit you perfectly, though it might not be all that easy to arrange at short notice. You are still taking excursions in your mind and your imagination is really working overtime. With everything to play for in sports and group interests your social life should be quite full.

4 SUNDAY
Moon Age Day 17   Moon Sign Libra

Make an early start and get stuck in for all you are worth. There are gains to be made in all areas of life and with the lunar high around there's no time to waste. It is quite likely that with just a little effort on your part today and tomorrow you can more than double your luck, and enjoy yourself too.

5 MONDAY
Moon Age Day 18   Moon Sign Libra

There is more than one way to achieve the progress you presently crave – and what's more you can rely on the good offices of others to help you out. This week should bring you the opportunity to get out of the house and to enjoy good company. Light-hearted in your approach to life, you are well worth knowing.

6 TUESDAY
Moon Age Day 19   Moon Sign Scorpio

Play it safe today, especially at work, and don't take anything for granted. What those around you think is the best way forward probably will not be your way to go and some conflict could arise as a result. If you are persuasive and use a psychological approach, you might avoid having to compromise.

7 WEDNESDAY
Moon Age Day 20   Moon Sign Scorpio

This is a period during which you can capitalise on all the effort you have put in previously. In other words you worked hard for what you are getting and now you deserve to reap the rewards. Others might not see things in quite this way but you are so persuasive at the moment you can bring anyone round to your point of view.

8 THURSDAY
Moon Age Day 21   Moon Sign Sagittarius

It might be difficult to get your message across today if others are refusing to listen to you. Keep calm, and if one method doesn't work try another. Start working more with people than with things and do your best to accommodate the differences you encounter, especially amongst work colleagues.

9 FRIDAY
Moon Age Day 22   Moon Sign Sagittarius

Though some aspects of your personal life might seem slightly unsettled, you are quite prepared to soldier on and to find solutions to little difficulties. Problems should not be overstated and in any case, there is a great deal of humour about. This makes you look at life in a very light-hearted but still realistic way.

10 SATURDAY   *Moon Age Day 23*   *Moon Sign Sagittarius*

Prospects look especially good for your personal finances, a subject which may occupy your thoughts today. It's good to plan, but don't let this stop you from making up your mind on the spur of the moment, especially in a romantic or social sense. Stand up for a family member who is having problems.

11 SUNDAY   *Moon Age Day 24*   *Moon Sign Capricorn*

Take a close look at your partner's needs today and do what you can to make life slightly easier for them. You seem to be quite helpful right across the board but you won't have much time for those who bleat about situations they could easily alter. Your confidence should remain high for a few days.

12 MONDAY   *Moon Age Day 25*   *Moon Sign Capricorn*

The social atmosphere around you at this time is likely to be varied and potentially exciting. Of course you will be contributing because nobody likes to mix and mingle more than Libra. You might discover that you have some sort of unexpected gift. It doesn't matter how silly it might seem – it's something new.

13 TUESDAY   *Moon Age Day 26*   *Moon Sign Aquarius*

Being at the centre of things is not a problem to you now – but then again, it rarely is. You show yourself off almost exactly as a good Libran should and you wear your originality like a badge of honour. Take something that is said about you with a pinch of salt because it isn't intended as any sort of insult.

14 WEDNESDAY   *Moon Age Day 27*   *Moon Sign Aquarius*

Now it is the workplace that is most favoured as you strive to streamline your working life. Impressing others on the way should not be at all difficult and your innovative attitude should be very welcome. People who have been having problems are likely to turn to you for advice and support, which you will be happy to offer.

15 THURSDAY   *Moon Age Day 28   Moon Sign Aquarius*

Prepare for tension in personal relationships and deal with it immediately. If there is any bone of contention between yourself and your partner it needs talking about and a compromise found. Don't leave anything to fester today because the quicker you are at sorting things out the happier you are going to be later.

16 FRIDAY   *Moon Age Day 29   Moon Sign Pisces*

It might be necessary to apply the brakes a little if you sense that some aspects of your life are getting out of control. In particular take care when it comes to personal attachments. There is just a small chance that your natural kindness is being misconstrued and that could lead to trouble later.

17 SATURDAY   *Moon Age Day 0   Moon Sign Pisces*

Places of luxury and enjoyment are likely to appeal to you greatly now and this Saturday marks an interlude when you will be less inclined to think about practical matters and more determined to spoil yourself in some way. Get together with friends to do something quite exciting, perhaps even slightly risqué.

18 SUNDAY   *Moon Age Day 1   Moon Sign Aries*

Today might get off to a fairly slow start and then the remainder of the day could seem to be a game of catch-up. Fortunately you will retain your sense of humour and you are unlikely to be too put out by the lunar low. Rely on the friends and family members when it comes to getting specific jobs done.

19 MONDAY   *Moon Age Day 2   Moon Sign Aries*

Making a good impression on others is not difficult, even though you might think you are blundering about like an idiot at the moment. This is not the case at all and although you can show your vulnerability at this time, it only makes others love you all the more. Your kind-hearted approach to life has never been more welcome.

20 TUESDAY
Moon Age Day 3   Moon Sign Aries

Although things might be slightly sluggish professionally, in a personal sense they really couldn't be better for Libra. You know how to hand out the compliments and these should be very well received. Your confidence to do the right thing remains essentially high but you might have some self-doubt.

21 WEDNESDAY
Moon Age Day 4   Moon Sign Taurus

It is unlikely that the really impulsive side of your nature is on display today and that turns out to be a good thing. A slightly low-key approach to most situations is what is presently called for. If there are problems somewhere within the family it is almost certain that you will be on hand to sort them out almost immediately.

22 THURSDAY
Moon Age Day 5   Moon Sign Taurus

The slightly wacky things that other people do won't upset you in the least. After all you come from what can be one of the zaniest signs of them all. You are original, inspirational, unusual and sometimes perhaps a little odd. All of this certainly gets you noticed and you enjoy playing to the crowd.

23 FRIDAY
☿ *Moon Age Day 6   Moon Sign Gemini*

Avoid important decisions for the moment or at least sidestep them until later. You don't have what it takes to impress people to the same extent you have been doing across the last few days and you probably don't want to. It isn't that you are miserable but you may well be happiest with your own company for now.

24 SATURDAY
☿ *Moon Age Day 7   Moon Sign Gemini*

Trends move on and now you are fully in the swing of things, almost from the moment you get out bed. What a difference a day makes, especially to an Air sign such as yours. Put new plans into action and you can also be fairly sure that other people will be quite happy to lend a hand. Romance looks especially good for today and tomorrow.

25 SUNDAY   ☿   *Moon Age Day 8   Moon Sign Cancer*

Where personal involvements are concerned there is just a small chance of some tension building up today. If there is something you have on your mind it would be better to speak out – albeit tactfully, because you won't gain anything by remaining silent. Friends may tax your patience too but not for long at a time.

26 MONDAY   ☿   *Moon Age Day 9   Moon Sign Cancer*

There is a small chance that you will be easily irritated by trivialities today and so it is likely that you will avoid them if at all possible. That's fine as far as it goes but unless you look at things carefully you might easily get into the odd scrape. Concentration is called for – but unfortunately so is a great deal of patience.

27 TUESDAY   ☿   *Moon Age Day 10   Moon Sign Leo*

Your home is likely to be the setting for social and romantic activities today, though you are still likely to be very busy in other ways too. Slowing life down might be the hardest thing to do but it is necessary on occasions. You don't want to miss a solid gold opportunity just because you aren't paying attention.

28 WEDNESDAY   ☿   *Moon Age Day 11   Moon Sign Leo*

The middle of the week may turn out to be the best time from a financial point of view. Not only are you dealing well with existing money but you also have good ideas about how you can get more in the weeks and months ahead. Share your inspiration with others because you could form an important partnership.

29 THURSDAY   ☿   *Moon Age Day 12   Moon Sign Virgo*

Don't be too quick to pick holes in someone else's idea. It is quite possible that what they are suggesting complements your own plans – even if you have to think about things a little in order to realise this. Things may not be what they seem and getting your detective head on could prove to be very informative.

30 FRIDAY ☿ *Moon Age Day 13 Moon Sign Virgo*

Remaining objective and in the main sensible, you have what it takes to get ahead steadily, but is that enough? It's a fact that Librans soon get bored unless something special is on the horizon. Maybe the time is right to start thinking about old things in new ways, not to mention making more of a physical effort.

31 SATURDAY ☿ *Moon Age Day 14 Moon Sign Libra*

The weekend should find you warm, attentive and especially kind to people who are less well off than you are. This charitable side to your nature will be well emphasised at this time and you will be doing everything you can to make the world a better place. Happiness comes from unexpected places today.

April

2018

1 SUNDAY ☿ *Moon Age Day 15   Moon Sign Libra*

You can make good progress today and the lunar high should prove to be supportive when it comes to monetary matters. Give yourself fully to enjoyment once the responsibilities of the day are out of the way and arrange for a change of scene if possible. You could be in the mood for a party if you can find one.

2 MONDAY ☿ *Moon Age Day 16   Moon Sign Scorpio*

There are opportunities at the moment for heart-to-heart talks and these might clear the air if there have been any misunderstandings recently. Make sure that you really listen to what people are saying, instead of hearing what you want to hear. At work you may have to rely on other people today.

3 TUESDAY ☿ *Moon Age Day 17   Moon Sign Scorpio*

You should find that you have the upper hand in talks and debates today – though there is nothing particularly surprising about that. Not everyone will agree with you, no matter how persuasive you manage to be and there are some people who will argue more or less on principle. Don't give in to negative thinking regarding new jobs.

4 WEDNESDAY ☿ *Moon Age Day 18   Moon Sign Scorpio*

Meetings, appointments and discussions are all important, relevant and keep you interested today. A new exchange of ideas should prove to be rewarding but you may have to think very carefully before you get yourself involved in some hobby or pastime that will tie you up a great deal.

5 THURSDAY ☿ *Moon Age Day 19   Moon Sign Sagittarius*

There could be some disputes to sort out within relationships and you may have difficulty enjoying the company of people you see as being too assertive. The trouble is there can only be one centre of attention at the moment and you may subconsciously think that should be you. Try to calm things down and be reasonable.

6 FRIDAY ☿ *Moon Age Day 20   Moon Sign Sagittarius*

Planetary trends favour your personal life now and you can make this a relaxing time if you opt for hearth and home. However, it might all be 'too' comfortable because there are other elements in your nature at the moment urging you to find excitement and even risk. Try to balance things out sensibly.

7 SATURDAY ☿ *Moon Age Day 21   Moon Sign Capricorn*

Professional plans could get re-routed as you spend more time sorting out domestic issues and personal wishes. You will be fulfilling your responsibilities well enough but if you are at work you might not take on quite as much responsibility as usual. Try to get a change of scenery at some time during today.

8 SUNDAY ☿ *Moon Age Day 22   Moon Sign Capricorn*

The time is right to follow your feelings regarding a personal issue. Family matters continue to be the main source of any rewards that come your way and you should have good reason to be proud of younger family members or your partner today. Don't take on a massive workload and find time today to move around freely.

9 MONDAY ☿ *Moon Age Day 23   Moon Sign Capricorn*

This could certainly be one of your better days for busy preparations or for getting out into the fresh air. The busiest Librans may not have even noticed that spring is now painting the hedgerows but it would do you good to get out and register this for yourself. You are soon going to enter a more dynamic phase, but for now relax.

10 TUESDAY ☿ *Moon Age Day 24   Moon Sign Aquarius*

There are likely to be some significant rewards around today but you may have to turn over a few stones in order to find them. Life can be quite eventful for Libra but it would also be easy to get bogged down with issues that you can't resolve easily. Keep it light and airy in your associations with others.

11 WEDNESDAY ☿ *Moon Age Day 25   Moon Sign Aquarius*

A change for the better probably lies in matters to do with hearth and home. There are discussions taking place to which you are an important contributor and you will be expected to speak honestly and with candour. Don't be too quick to take offence today if friends seem to be insulting you in some way. They probably aren't.

12 THURSDAY ☿   *Moon Age Day 26   Moon Sign Pisces*

Current influences are likely to go your way as far as your social life is concerned but you could be crossing swords with those who have egos as big as yours at the moment. When you think you are merely sticking up for yourself you could actually be getting on your high horse. The more you laugh today the better.

13 FRIDAY   ☿   *Moon Age Day 27   Moon Sign Pisces*

At work you should find yourself happy to co-operate and more willing than ever to take on new responsibilities, even if some of these are a little scary at first. People are keen to rely on you and to trust your judgement and this makes you behave even more responsibly. Your love life could also be taking a turn for the better.

14 SATURDAY   ☿   *Moon Age Day 28   Moon Sign Pisces*

You would be very wise to keep abreast of all news and views today because there is information around that could be of great use to you. You cannot be sure at the moment just what is going to be significant, so it is important to pay attention. The more you do so, the greater the rewards.

♎

15 SUNDAY
Moon Age Day 29   Moon Sign Aries

With the lunar low arriving you will be less inclined to push yourself or to put yourself forward in company. For the moment you will be happy to be an 'also ran' even though this is usually quite contrary to your nature. Despite the quiet interlude it is possible that you are still in demand with others.

16 MONDAY
Moon Age Day 0   Moon Sign Aries

Keep a low profile, get on with something fairly simple and hum a little song. That's the best way to deal with the lunar low. When you are not doing practical things you might decide to read a good book or magazine and to put your feet up for once. Allow family pressures to flow over you or let someone else sort them out.

17 TUESDAY
Moon Age Day 1   Moon Sign Taurus

This is a favourable time for family and domestic issues. Although you are still likely to be very busy, you can find the hours necessary to concentrate on matters you might have been putting off or to one side recently. It's amazing how capable you are at this time, and just how much you can actually get done.

18 WEDNESDAY
Moon Age Day 2   Moon Sign Taurus

Quite original ideas occupy your mind under present planetary trends and doing things in the normal way won't seem to be all that appealing. To be original is part of what you are about and so is fine, but there are occasions when tried and tested methods still work best. It's up to you to establish when this is the case.

19 THURSDAY
Moon Age Day 3   Moon Sign Gemini

This could be a period during which you are rethinking some of your former strategies and wondering if you got something right. Perhaps this has to do with a relationship but it could equally be something associated with work. There is certainly plenty of curiosity around now, plus a tendency to dig quite deep for answers.

20 FRIDAY
Moon Age Day 4   Moon Sign Gemini

It is possible that there will be some good news coming in from afar and you would respond to this in a very positive way. Despite the fact that mundane issues hold you back, you seem to be very progressive and more than willing to put in whatever effort is necessary in order to get where you want to be.

21 SATURDAY
Moon Age Day 5   Moon Sign Cancer

Friends might think you are rather too assertive for your own good but if they know you well, this is something for which they will readily forgive you. Yours is an Air sign and it relies a great deal on communication, both given and received. It is worth remembering that today because it is words that will see you getting on well.

22 SUNDAY
Moon Age Day 6   Moon Sign Cancer

The community spirit is likely to be quite strong and you will want to join in as much as possible with events taking place at or close to where you live. The year is moving on and as the weather improves you might have a hankering to spend more time out of doors. Perhaps go out for a walk if you can.

23 MONDAY
Moon Age Day 7   Moon Sign Leo

You may not be as receptive as usual when it comes to the point of view of others – even those you are quite willing to listen to as a rule. You think you have all the answers and that can be a mistake. It doesn't matter how old or experienced you are, there is always something important that you can learn today.

24 TUESDAY
Moon Age Day 8   Moon Sign Leo

Your willpower is now very strong – so much so that it would take a good person to hold you back in any way. You will be efficient and sure to put in only what effort is necessary in each case. Libra is always discriminating, but never more so than at the moment. This leads both to expected and surprising successes.

25 WEDNESDAY   *Moon Age Day 9   Moon Sign Virgo*

With good trends prevailing, it looks as though your love life will continue in a generally positive way, especially if you are at the start of a new relationship. In any dispute at work, be willing to give ground. It won't hurt you to do so and your colleagues will respect you all the more for your attitude.

26 THURSDAY   *Moon Age Day 10   Moon Sign Virgo*

It is possible that other people will be throwing their weight about today. If that means relatives, you should be able to shrug your shoulders and carry on pretty much as normal. It might be more difficult to deal with if this happens at work, but if you have any sense, you will not allow yourself to be provoked.

27 FRIDAY   *Moon Age Day 11   Moon Sign Virgo*

Look for ways and means to enhance your domestic life and you can also make relatives happy on the way. You might have a particular worry about someone in particular, but look at this in a detached manner if you can. Ask yourself what advice you would offer to a friend and then take the advice yourself.

28 SATURDAY   *Moon Age Day 12   Moon Sign Libra*

You are a very positive person to be with at the best of times but especially so while the lunar high is running the show. Your talent for inspiring other people is always noteworthy but is especially strong at the present time. This can be of tremendous use when it comes to getting on at work and for seeking any form of advancement.

29 SUNDAY   *Moon Age Day 13   Moon Sign Libra*

Good luck is still on your side and you can rely on your positive frame of mind to get you what you want for at least some of today. You tend to be extremely enterprising in your ideas and the fact that it is so easy to get others on board really helps every situation. Plan now for travel immediately or later on.

30 MONDAY

Moon Age Day 14   Moon Sign Scorpio

You may experience a few difficulties in the practical world, if only because you are tempted to do something ill-advised or poorly thought-out. Fools rush in where angels fear to tread – and it's possible you will come unstuck if you don't heed this advice. Don't expect it to be easy for a Libran, though.

May

1 TUESDAY
Moon Age Day 15   Moon Sign Scorpio

Social commitments could make significant demands upon you and there may simply not be enough time to do everything you would wish today. This being the case, you will need to look carefully at all matters and prioritise the most important. After that, stick to what you have decided and don't deviate.

2 WEDNESDAY
Moon Age Day 16   Moon Sign Sagittarius

You could now be challenged to overcome selfish tendencies and to show just how charitable and giving you are capable of being. For perhaps the first time this year the really quirky side of Libra begins to show. Some people would describe you as eccentric but labels of this sort will only make you laugh.

3 THURSDAY
Moon Age Day 17   Moon Sign Sagittarius

It's time to try out some new ideas and to be bold and enterprising in almost everything you do. Get involved in some interesting discussions and show those you are talking to just how intelligent you can be. You can learn much about the world today by simply keeping your eyes and ears open.

4 FRIDAY
Moon Age Day 18   Moon Sign Sagittarius

There is now likely to be a strong emphasis on personal and family concerns. Outside obligations are put on hold for a while as you respond to present planetary trends. Focus your efforts on acting quickly in situations that you know instinctively could work well for you in the future.

5 SATURDAY   *Moon Age Day 19   Moon Sign Capricorn*

The planetary influences around you at this time will stir up restless feelings and the need for fun and romance is paramount. This can be easily fulfilled and so can your desire to widen your immediate friendship circle. There ought to be plenty of energy around and some new and boisterous pastime is not out of the question.

6 SUNDAY   *Moon Age Day 20   Moon Sign Capricorn*

Don't change your mind regarding a practical matter and do what you can to reorganise things at home, if required. This is a good time for communications of all sorts and you might be especially busy on the computer or with text messages. New skills are learned very easily under present trends.

7 MONDAY   *Moon Age Day 21   Moon Sign Aquarius*

Anything to do with your career or practical matters is inclined to be looking much better at this time. You are filled with a great sense of purpose and a desire to get on side with people you recognise as being life's winners. Shining out like a star, you can fill a room with your charisma and you make many friends on your journey now.

8 TUESDAY   *Moon Age Day 22   Moon Sign Aquarius*

Keep any self-righteous behaviour at bay and don't either think or pretend that you have all the answers. If you are willing to ask for advice people will do everything they can to help you out. Standard responses to the enquiries of family members might not be enough to satisfy them and you may need to be quite ingenious.

9 WEDNESDAY   *Moon Age Day 23   Moon Sign Aquarius*

There are forces at work that seem to be helping you get what you want right now, especially where practical matters are concerned. Jobs that usually take an age can be sorted out in a fraction of the usual time and everything falls into place quite readily. This leaves you with time on your hands that you might want to use socially.

♎

10 THURSDAY *Moon Age Day 24   Moon Sign Pisces*

Expect a high spot on the domestic scene and less aggravation and worry at home than might have been the case for a month or two. You may not feel inclined to move around much for the next few days because you are getting most of your enjoyment close to home. Invite friends round and enjoy socialising.

11 FRIDAY *Moon Age Day 25   Moon Sign Pisces*

Newer and better chances come along in terms of your financial planning and you seem to be able to make gains at every turn. Some friendships might be up and down but this is probably no fault of yours. The time is probably right for new attachments to come along – perhaps even people you used to know in the dim and distant past.

12 SATURDAY *Moon Age Day 26   Moon Sign Aries*

Life might seem somewhat dreary today but it really depends on the way you approach the lunar low. If you keep an open mind and refuse to get down in the dumps about things that are not of any real importance you may barely notice this planetary visit. Try different responses to the same old problems.

13 SUNDAY *Moon Age Day 27   Moon Sign Aries*

This could be a fairly taxing day in some ways but the same advice as yesterday still holds good. Pretend you are feeling extremely positive and use your imagination to solve any immediate concerns you could have. With ingenuity and enterprise you can turn rain clouds inside out. This evening can be especially heart warming.

14 MONDAY *Moon Age Day 28   Moon Sign Taurus*

You now seem to be making all the right moves when it comes to being noticed. Life hands you a few favours without you having to do anything to inspire them and good luck is inclined to follow you around like a shadow for a few days. For the moment you should be especially happy in your love life and anxious to show your romantic side.

15 TUESDAY
Moon Age Day 0   Moon Sign Taurus

Brand new romantic developments are favoured and planetary trends put you in the right place to benefit from personal attachments. Finding the right words to let someone know how you feel isn't generally difficult for you but at the moment it's a piece of cake. Get together with people you don't see too often if that is possible.

16 WEDNESDAY
Moon Age Day 1   Moon Sign Gemini

Family members will now probably be doing their utmost to make you feel comfortable and happy. Not everything they attempt will entirely suit you because in some situations you hate too much fuss. In professional matters you should definitely be on a roll and well able to keep up with any proposed changes.

17 THURSDAY
Moon Age Day 2   Moon Sign Gemini

Communicating your ideas is not difficult today – let's face it, as a Libran it rarely is a problem. The difference now is that almost everyone will be willing to listen and you are attractive to others. This generally means you get a favourable response from every direction – even ones you would never expect.

18 FRIDAY
Moon Age Day 3   Moon Sign Cancer

Romance and leisure activities receive positive planetary support, though it is also clear that you won't suffer fools gladly at the moment so woe betide anyone who crosses you at work. There is quite a marked difference at the moment between the way you behave socially and what can be expected of you professionally.

19 SATURDAY
Moon Age Day 4   Moon Sign Cancer

There appears to be a high degree of nervous energy about today and you might be quite jangly in some ways. This happens to Air signs such as Libra but it isn't necessarily a bad thing. It is easy to get the hormones flowing, either for sporting activities or in personal relationships.

20 SUNDAY
Moon Age Day 5   Moon Sign Leo

Chaos surrounds you at the moment, though on the whole it seems to be affecting others rather than you. As a result you may be called upon to offer assistance on a number of occasions. The fact that you are still nervy could get in the way of normal progress but life should be fairly routine in most respects.

21 MONDAY
Moon Age Day 6   Moon Sign Leo

Take care to make sure that your thinking does not become inflexible. Perhaps it is time to broaden your outlook in some respects and you might also decide that you need a change of some sort. Travel is not out of the question, or at the very least planning a journey that will take place at some time later in the year.

22 TUESDAY
Moon Age Day 7   Moon Sign Leo

This is a period when you will probably have very little time to spend on yourself. This is because you are thinking so much about everyone else and putting yourself out repeatedly; but the strange thing is that the more you do, the greater will be the blessings you notice. Libra is more or less totally unselfish now.

23 WEDNESDAY
Moon Age Day 8   Moon Sign Virgo

Now you need to make extra space in your work schedule as you are likely to have a good deal more to do than you may have expected. Bosses and people in authority might now change their minds regularly and this has a bearing on your own life. This is the start of what could turn out to be a very busy time.

24 THURSDAY
Moon Age Day 9   Moon Sign Virgo

This is a great time to be involved in group events and to get involved in projects that help you meet new people. The busier you are, the happier you seem to be and you may also experience much in the way of general good fortune. It's as if things seem to fall into place more or less of their own accord.

25 FRIDAY · *Moon Age Day 10 · Moon Sign Libra*

Along comes the lunar high and with it better luck and more instant gratification. In areas of your life that have been somewhat static or tedious recently you will now be injecting more fun and greater enthusiasm. Almost anything you decide to do at the moment is likely to work out fine, even when you know you are taking risks.

26 SATURDAY · *Moon Age Day 11 · Moon Sign Libra*

Someone might be more than willing to do you a great favour today and you certainly can't do yourself any harm by asking them. It's amazing how cheeky you can be under the influence of the lunar high but this should turn out to be a positive thing. People love to have you around because you are such fun.

27 SUNDAY · *Moon Age Day 12 · Moon Sign Scorpio*

Domestic relationships fall into the spotlight in a big way under present trends. There is something quite powerful going on, so react carefully to the way others are behaving. In some situations you may not be fully in the picture and you will need to ask a few leading questions in order to fully understand.

28 MONDAY · *Moon Age Day 13 · Moon Sign Scorpio*

At home you should say what you think, even on those occasions when you wonder if others will approve. You could be really surprised at the reaction you get and there are some pleasant interludes in store for most Librans at this time. There are moments when you are happy to wear your heart on your sleeve.

29 TUESDAY · *Moon Age Day 14 · Moon Sign Sagittarius*

You want to assert yourself today – but how to go about it without upsetting someone? Whilst this is clearly a question you will be asking yourself, you don't really need to worry too much about it. Having taken this matter on board, you have already dealt with it in a sense. Save some time today to nothing in particular.

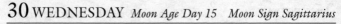

30 WEDNESDAY *Moon Age Day 15* *Moon Sign Sagittarius*

You are short on patience today and so perhaps you should avoid trivial matters. There are certain things that look good but which soon lose their shine. The more important the task you are undertaking, the better is your chance to make situations come good for you. One job at a time, that's the secret.

31 THURSDAY *Moon Age Day 16* *Moon Sign Sagittarius*

You are as busy as could be today, throwing yourself into a new day with all the energy you possibly can. Don't be in the least surprised if people are picking up on your infectious sense of humour. You could be singled out for special treatment by someone you didn't even consider a friend only a short while ago.

2018

1 FRIDAY
Moon Age Day 17   Moon Sign Capricorn

This is a time during which you can probably make progress with less effort than might usually be the case. You should also have something to smile about as far as your career is concerned and you appear to be turning heads in a positive way wherever you go. This is Libra showing itself at its very best.

2 SATURDAY
Moon Age Day 18   Moon Sign Capricorn

Any sort of high-profile situation would suit you today and you get more or less what you want because of the force of your personality. Though you are likely to be very generous to others you might not always be getting the best from them but you won't worry too much as long as you have control over your own destiny in the main.

3 SUNDAY
Moon Age Day 19   Moon Sign Aquarius

This is a good period for developing your practical strengths, especially at work. Of course this might not be possible on a Sunday, but you also have your planning head on and will be quite happy to sort things out in your mind ahead of a new push later. You might be thinking about travelling, either now or very soon.

4 MONDAY
Moon Age Day 20   Moon Sign Aquarius

Some success looks likely at work, and you can make a good impression when it counts. If not everyone is keen to follow your lead, concentrate on the people who are and don't waste time on lost causes. In terms of finances you need to look carefully at investments and probably should not sign contracts for the next day or two.

5 TUESDAY
Moon Age Day 21   Moon Sign Aquarius

Comfort and security could definitely be on your agenda, though not significantly, and it is clear that you are still willing to take the odd risk, at least for today. You might find that the way you approach others needs some modification if someone does not respond in the way you would normally expect.

6 WEDNESDAY
Moon Age Day 22   Moon Sign Pisces

There isn't much doubt about your creative drive, or your present ability to get things right first time. You do need change and diversity if you are not to become bored by the same old routines and you can't expect to be satisfied with the everyday. If you don't ring the changes you will find that restlessness is the result.

7 THURSDAY
Moon Age Day 23   Moon Sign Pisces

With a good talent for delegating work, it won't be difficult for you to get other people to follow your instructions. It's a fact that more of your time this week is being spent supervising others, both at work and at home, rather than actually getting stuck in yourself. The way you look will really matter to you at this time.

8 FRIDAY
Moon Age Day 24   Moon Sign Aries

This is a time for rest and reflection because the more you try to move forward at a pace, the stickier things could seem. The lunar low should not make you depressed because, after all, it only lasts for a couple of days. Keep a sense of proportion and don't get carried away with pointless worries or even fantasies.

9 SATURDAY
Moon Age Day 25   Moon Sign Aries

You are now at your best where your love life is concerned but you will almost certainly find that making any sort of practical progress is impossible. Opt for the simple and don't make waves in relationships. This is the best time of the month to stand and watch things happen rather than getting yourself too involved.

10 SUNDAY   *Moon Age Day 26   Moon Sign Aries*

Capitalise on new opportunities that come your way and explore new methods of getting ahead in both a personal and a professional way. You are very good at mixing business with pleasure and especially so under present planetary trends. New social avenues should also be opening up and these become more obvious later in the day.

11 MONDAY   *Moon Age Day 27   Moon Sign Taurus*

This might be one of the best days of the month professionally because it looks as though things are going to fall into line quite easily. In a personal sense you will have great sex appeal and an ability to turn heads more or less wherever you go. This can be very gratifying but could also prove embarrassing at times.

12 TUESDAY   *Moon Age Day 28   Moon Sign Taurus*

Look ahead towards some happy social situations and make the most of what a summer Tuesday has to offer. Under present trends you will not wish to be held back or kept in the same place for long. The Air-sign qualities of Libra are now really on show and these demand that you mix and mingle just as much as possible.

13 WEDNESDAY   *Moon Age Day 0   Moon Sign Gemini*

Concentrate on whatever field you understand the best today. This is not because you fail to show an interest in life across the board, merely that you are presently at your most potent. In a professional sense it appears that you cannot put a foot wrong and you just seem to have 'it' – whatever it might be.

14 THURSDAY   *Moon Age Day 1   Moon Sign Gemini*

You can deal with many and varied issues whilst the planets occupy their present positions. There isn't much doubt now about your Libran credentials and you display yourself at your very best – especially in the way you look. Keep abreast of local news and get involved in things that are happening in your vicinity.

15 FRIDAY
Moon Age Day 2   Moon Sign Cancer

Dealings with others are likely to be pleasant and rewarding, which leaves you feeling fairly satisfied with your lot in life. Much of this has to do with the charm you are exuding more or less wherever you go and you will always have a smile on your face. People find you easy to relate to.

16 SATURDAY
Moon Age Day 3   Moon Sign Cancer

You seem to be heading towards the end of a particular chapter in your life, which for some will come as a relief. When one door closes another opens and this is certainly going to be the case for you. Libra never hangs around for long and you are likely to move forward progressively in the days ahead.

17 SUNDAY
Moon Age Day 4   Moon Sign Leo

Life can be inspirational, especially when you look around and see the many opportunities that stand before you at this time. With the summer here and even more good weather to come, you should be feeling on top of the world. Don't get involved in petty disagreements, especially at work. You don't have time for them.

18 MONDAY
Moon Age Day 5   Moon Sign Leo

Your sympathetic nature could be aroused at this time, bringing you in touch with those who are in need of your compassion and your solid support. Your ego is less prominent than it has been and this makes everyone love you all the more. Even though you are gentler in your approach you can still get your own way.

19 TUESDAY
Moon Age Day 6   Moon Sign Virgo

Minor, possibly unexpected pressures are likely to stop you in your tracks at some stage during the morning but the general direction is onward and upward. There might be moments when you have to drop everything you were doing and get on with something different, if only so that you can bring help and relief to someone else.

20 WEDNESDAY   *Moon Age Day 7   Moon Sign Virgo*

Though you seem to be very much on top of most practical issues, when it comes to the personal side of life you are likely to be having a few small problems. People don't behave or react as you would expect and although you are a deeply intuitive person, for the moment your instincts could fail you a little.

21 THURSDAY   *Moon Age Day 8   Moon Sign Libra*

The Moon is now back in your sign and brings with it one of the most potent lunar highs you are likely to experience this year. With the Sun in its present position you will be raring to go and enjoying everything that life has to offer. It's a fact of life that if people can't keep up with your pace at the moment they will be left behind.

22 FRIDAY   *Moon Age Day 9   Moon Sign Libra*

There is good scope for personal gain right now and you will probably find more money coming in. This is likely to be as much as a result of good fortune as sensible planning, though you are quite ingenious too. If you want to shine when you are in the public eye you couldn't pick a better time to do so than now.

23 SATURDAY   *Moon Age Day 10   Moon Sign Scorpio*

The pace of life and communications with others both keep you extremely active this weekend and there might be something that has to be finished ahead of Sunday that seems to take forever to do. Once you are freed from practical restrictions you should really explode into a fascinating and pleasing social life.

24 SUNDAY   *Moon Age Day 11   Moon Sign Scorpio*

Your social life and also romance offer the best chance of interest on this particular Sunday. It looks as though you are getting yourself ready for a journey, or at least planning for one later, and in the meantime short outings are also likely. If there is one thing you won't want to do at the moment, it's to be restricted in any way.

25 MONDAY   *Moon Age Day 12   Moon Sign Scorpio*

This should be a really excellent time for Libra, particularly in your personal or love life. Plan to have something big happen today and if that isn't possible, make a special fuss of almost everyone you encounter. It is so easy for you now to make the most of the natural gifts you have inherited – in fact you are a real winner.

26 TUESDAY   *Moon Age Day 13   Moon Sign Sagittarius*

This is another good period for gathering together useful information and for finding ways to use it to your best advantage and for that of others. People still love to have you around, in fact there is rarely a time when they do not. A slight tiff with a friend isn't out of the question, especially if they behave in an untypical way.

27 WEDNESDAY   *Moon Age Day 14   Moon Sign Sagittarius*

You will feel better and get more done when you work alone today. This is because your level of patience isn't quite what it has been. You now need to rediscover the details of something you had more or less forgotten and to put them into practice for the future. Some amazing coincidences are also likely.

28 THURSDAY   *Moon Age Day 15   Moon Sign Capricorn*

Your ego is to the fore at the moment and there are some people who could think you are very slightly arrogant in your approach. In truth you are merely confident and that should ensure that you make rapid progress, especially at work. All the same, showing a little humility at some stage would not be a bad thing.

29 FRIDAY   *Moon Age Day 16   Moon Sign Capricorn*

The opportunity for happy times comes from some quite unexpected directions and also from friends who have new and fascinating plans. Get involved in what others are doing and add your own opinions to those of colleagues or friends. At home you are likely to remain extremely active and quite innovative.

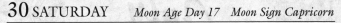

30 SATURDAY   *Moon Age Day 17   Moon Sign Capricorn*

Confidence and charm are in ready supply and you make a big impact wherever you happen to go. The focus of life when you are not working is likely to be squarely on love and you have what it takes to make others look your way. People find you fascinating at the moment and also just a little mysterious.

July

2018

1 SUNDAY
Moon Age Day 18   Moon Sign Aquarius

The emphasis now turns towards partnerships, especially those that have a romantic dimension. It isn't hard for you to make friends and influence people at the moment and in fact there might be occasions when you consider you are too popular for your own good. Finding moments to do things on your own could be difficult.

2 MONDAY
Moon Age Day 19   Moon Sign Aquarius

New trends arise today and some of these will probably make you think again about issues you thought you understood only too well. It is really a question of applying new insight into your present and future plans because you seem to be extremely intuitive at the moment. Not everyone will want to co-operate with you today.

3 TUESDAY
Moon Age Day 20   Moon Sign Pisces

You have a good eye for details and it pains you if something is not the way you think it should be. However, other people have a point of view as well and it might be best all round if you don't interfere too much for the moment. Try to avoid exhausting yourself by trying to get everything done at the same time and take some rest.

4 WEDNESDAY
Moon Age Day 21   Moon Sign Pisces

Things that have been building up for a long time can now either reach a definite conclusion or else suddenly fade away without any real cause. As a result there are both pleasant surprises and less pleasant ones to be encountered. Even when things don't work out as you would wish there should always be sensible alternatives.

5 THURSDAY
Moon Age Day 22   Moon Sign Pisces

It looks as though emotional relationships will provide your warmest and most enjoyable contacts for the moment. Look to the people who genuinely know you the best and who will be quite happy to do more or less anything for you. You may also be calling in a few favours from especially good and cherished friends.

6 FRIDAY
Moon Age Day 23   Moon Sign Aries

This is likely to be a rather sluggish time and one when a half-hearted approach is most likely on your part. This is something you can't really avoid while the lunar low is present but you can at least rely on others to push situations forward on your behalf. Your own personal energy might be flagging but that of your friends isn't.

7 SATURDAY
Moon Age Day 24   Moon Sign Aries

The planetary lull patch is likely to continue and you may feel less enthusiastic about life than would generally be the case. Be patient with yourself and with the world at large because these less-than-favourable trends won't extend far beyond today. Look after cash right now and don't spend lavishly.

8 SUNDAY
Moon Age Day 25   Moon Sign Taurus

You should now find favourable circumstances coming along, especially when it comes to your contacts with friends and acquaintances. Plan ahead in order to have something special happening and do whatever you can to get family members motivated. Make out of doors activities a must.

9 MONDAY
Moon Age Day 26   Moon Sign Taurus

There should be plenty happening in personal attachments and you will be happy to take part in social events too. The only thing that could get put on the back-burner for the moment is work because there doesn't seem to be all that much time to fit it in. Newer and better means of making money are coming but not for a few days.

10 TUESDAY · *Moon Age Day 27 · Moon Sign Gemini*

Things should now be looking better on the monetary front, especially if you are in business. Added securities are likely to come from the direction of your partner and you are about to enjoy a very comfortable and more certain time as far as love is concerned. Your expectations might not be quite as high as they have been, so all this will be a bonus.

11 WEDNESDAY · *Moon Age Day 28 · Moon Sign Gemini*

There could be plenty to keep you happy and enthusiastic during the middle of the week, though you may not be making the progress you would wish, probably because other people are proving somehow difficult. Fortunately you can smile at the odd mishap and allow nature to take its course. In other words you are well in command.

12 THURSDAY · *Moon Age Day 29 · Moon Sign Cancer*

Libra tends to be very self-sufficient at the moment and you won't require a great deal from the world outside. On the contrary you prefer to make your own decisions and would be far happier if people don't interfere in decisions you see as being entirely your own. Going it alone is not usually Libran but seems to be right now.

13 FRIDAY · *Moon Age Day 0 · Moon Sign Cancer*

Favourable highlights come along through personal relationships and as a result of your ability to move around and to make the best of the summer weather. When it comes to impressing people with your natural charm you should have no difficulty whatsoever. Don't be too quick to pass judgement on the actions of a casual acquaintance.

14 SATURDAY · *Moon Age Day 1 · Moon Sign Leo*

For much of the time today you are likely to be highly industrious and you won't easily be diverted from any course of action you have decided to follow. It isn't that you are being stubborn, simply that you are moving at such a pace you won't really be in the market for advice. Socially speaking you may need to slow things down a little.

15 SUNDAY · *Moon Age Day 2 · Moon Sign Leo*

At what could appear to be a very crucial stage of your life you could find yourself being quite indecisive. In order to react more instinctively and positively you will need to feel that your own thoughts are actually worth something. This might be slightly difficult if you feel that certain people are ignoring your point of view.

16 MONDAY · *Moon Age Day 3 · Moon Sign Virgo*

This is definitely a time to exploit the best possibilities of your love life. It may be in full bloom during the coming week and there isn't any doubt about the way you are able to captivate that one, very special person. The depth of your affection knows no bounds and this extends to all those you care about.

17 TUESDAY · *Moon Age Day 4 · Moon Sign Virgo*

Where work issues are concerned, getting ahead at the moment has a great deal to do with being in the know. For this reason it is definitely worthwhile listening and watching even more than you normally might. Even the most casual remarks could have far-reaching implications and may lead you to formulate new strategies.

18 WEDNESDAY · *Moon Age Day 5 · Moon Sign Libra*

You seem to have the edge now when it comes to decision-making and the arrival of the lunar high comes just in time for you to play a major role in new situations that are about to unfold. Most of the negativity that has surrounded you for a few days is blown away on a wind of change and you are about as reactive and positive as ever.

19 THURSDAY · *Moon Age Day 6 · Moon Sign Libra*

You should experience positive trends in both your personal and your professional life and you will also be taking part in some potentially exciting social possibilities. Travel is well highlighted at this time and you can certainly benefit from any change of scene, whether it was planned ages ago or has just been decided upon today.

20 FRIDAY
Moon Age Day 7   Moon Sign Libra

Keep track of everything that is happening around you and don't be tardy when it comes to making those important moves that mean you stay ahead of the field. What matters the most at present is your ability to match practical skills to the level of popularity you are enjoying at present. This combination keeps you succeeding.

21 SATURDAY
Moon Age Day 8   Moon Sign Scorpio

Now is the time to gain from all kinds of input and information. Do make sure though that you are not simply gathering ideas together just for the sake of doing so. After preparation comes action and you won't get any prizes for thinking what might work best. It is important at present to have the courage of your convictions.

22 SUNDAY
Moon Age Day 9   Moon Sign Scorpio

You tend to have a very unique style when it comes to living your life and that is part of what makes you so popular with others. Your charm is turned up to full and few people will find it easy to avoid or ignore your magnetic personality. Don't worry about being a little eccentric. That's another reason people like you.

23 MONDAY
Moon Age Day 10   Moon Sign Sagittarius

Conflicts could be the order of the day as far as your home life is concerned, which may be part of the reason you are now more committed to your work and to all practical matters. You may not be the one who is creating difficulties but it looks as though you will be the one who is expected to sort them out.

24 TUESDAY
Moon Age Day 11   Moon Sign Sagittarius

Look towards a socially uplifting time, both today and for several more days to come. What you learn when you are mixing with others could prove to be invaluable further down the line and you are more than willing to put in any amount of effort to ensure your popularity remains intact. Your love life can shine like a star today.

25 WEDNESDAY *Moon Age Day 12 Moon Sign Capricorn*

This is not a day when you need to worry about money or the general progress you are making in life. It would be far more satisfying under present trends to mix with others whenever you have a few moments to spare, and to keep busy. Unnecessary worries will creep in on those occasions you sit around and ruminate.

26 THURSDAY *Moon Age Day 13 Moon Sign Capricorn*

Don't get so hooked up on the idea of making money that you begin to forget what is really important in your life. It is love and affection that really counts today and you won't have any trouble proving how much you care. Aspects of your social life can be quite racy but you remain well in control of your emotions under all circumstances.

27 FRIDAY *Moon Age Day 14 Moon Sign Capricorn*

This is a time of potentially wonderful events, some of which come like a bolt from the blue. Romance is high on your agenda and Librans who have been looking for a new love should focus their efforts around now. New opportunities surround you on all sides and even if you can't make your move yet you will be planning seriously.

28 SATURDAY *Moon Age Day 15 Moon Sign Aquarius*

Although you might appear to be slightly pushy today this is only because you want the very best for everyone. Of course people generally can't be expected to read your mind so it is vitally important for you to explain yourself whenever the opportunity to do so arises. Not everyone will be impressed with you today but carry on anyway.

29 SUNDAY *Moon Age Day 16 Moon Sign Aquarius*

It is now towards your emotional and love life that your mind is apt to turn. Your relationships with others can take a turn for the better, mainly because you are so accommodating. Pointless rules and regulations are inclined to get on your nerves, which is why you will be more than happy to ignore at least some of them.

30 MONDAY
Moon Age Day 17   Moon Sign Pisces

Avoid unnecessary assumptions today and rely on the evidence that stands before you. This is a good time to be slightly cautious about your health but not worrisome. There are measures you can take to improve your physical condition and these should be tried before you start thinking you are ill. Libra often worries far too much.

31 TUESDAY
Moon Age Day 18   Moon Sign Pisces

You now have a confident and optimistic outlook and this trend could see a turning point in your fortunes. So strong is your personality at the moment that people around you will not question your values or ideas and should be more than willing to do your bidding. Colleagues in particular are likely to trust you in almost any situation.

August

2018

1 WEDNESDAY ☿ *Moon Age Day 19 Moon Sign Pisces*

Enlist the co-operation of colleagues and friends. The input you receive from others may well light the path towards success. You are at your very best when it comes to sharing but there are certain aspects of life that you won't allow anyone to get too close to. This is an unusual trait – but then so is Libra.

2 THURSDAY ☿ *Moon Age Day 20 Moon Sign Aries*

You might now find it wise to wind down a few of your efforts for a couple of days. The lunar low will take the wind from your sails and might make it extra difficult for you to get what you want from life in a material sense. Fortunately these restrictions are short-lived, though you may also feel out of sorts emotionally at present.

3 FRIDAY ☿ *Moon Age Day 21 Moon Sign Aries*

This is not a day for making much in the way of gains, especially in a financial sense. You might have to make do with second-best in some situations and it might also be quite hard to enlist the support you really need. Later in the day things should be improving and can look very much better on the personal scene by the evening.

4 SATURDAY ☿ *Moon Age Day 22 Moon Sign Taurus*

Communication increases with curiosity at the moment and this is a trend that lightens your life no end. Today offers change and diversity, plus the chance to enjoy the summer weather and to get more fresh air. How about a picnic or a barbecue? As long as the company is good it doesn't really matter what you decide to do.

5 SUNDAY ☿ *Moon Age Day 23   Moon Sign Taurus*

Feel free to express yourself and if you find yourself involved in situations that are repressive or which force you to take an opposing point of view to your own natural inclinations, get out of them. Nothing could be worse for you at the moment that to feel squashed by circumstances or bullied by anyone.

6 MONDAY ☿ *Moon Age Day 24   Moon Sign Gemini*

Though practical matters should go smoothly enough you could be something of a hard taskmaster in terms of what you expect from other people. This might be a professional issue or even something that is happening at home. Try to make the jobs you hand out as much fun as possible and balance enjoyment with hard work.

7 TUESDAY ☿ *Moon Age Day 25   Moon Sign Gemini*

A new and more profitable period is on the way, especially where your social life is concerned. Getting to know new people is likely to be fun and you have all it takes to open up important new avenues in friendship. If your love life isn't exactly what you would wish this could be the best time to work at creating a little more oomph.

8 WEDNESDAY ☿ *Moon Age Day 26   Moon Sign Gemini*

Your mind is now working at super-fast speed and you will have a tendency to express yourself in a rather hurried manner. As a result you could make some mistakes or give a less than favourable impression of yourself. Slow things down a little and make a conscious effort not to be running around from pillar to post.

9 THURSDAY ☿ *Moon Age Day 27   Moon Sign Cancer*

Simple talks with friends are what you are looking for today and certainly nothing too deep, intellectual or philosophical. You are presently taking what some might call a superficial view of life but that's fine for the moment. While others are studious and enmeshed in detail you can skip along in bare feet, humming a little tune.

10 FRIDAY ☿ *Moon Age Day 28   Moon Sign Cancer*

Personal relationships should now be very fulfilling and you are looking extremely attractive when viewed through the eyes of other people. The time is right to break out, but probably not until Monday. For the moment play it cool and show someone you are interested, but without going over the top.

11 SATURDAY ☿ *Moon Age Day 0   Moon Sign Leo*

For much of the time right now you will be getting out and about and meeting some very interesting people. Some of them, while starting out as social contacts, could prove to be extremely important to you in a professional or financial way. It's worth cultivating some new interests under these trends.

12 SUNDAY ☿ *Moon Age Day 1   Moon Sign Leo*

Some professional opinions could prove boring or less than relevant today. In any case this is, after all, a Sunday so whether you are working or not you must find at least some time for personal enjoyment. Dump all the practical concerns for a few hours and find newer and better ways to let your hair down.

13 MONDAY ☿ *Moon Age Day 2   Moon Sign Virgo*

Seize a chance whenever you can and don't be worried if that means leaving behind something that has been with you for a very long time. This might be something material but is much more likely to be a now redundant attitude or a judgement about yourself that is turning out to be far from the truth. Look after money today.

14 TUESDAY ☿ *Moon Age Day 3   Moon Sign Virgo*

If you take your own ideas and opinions too much for granted you could fall out with others as a result. There is definitely a way to get what you want, whilst at the same time convincing those around you that you have listened very carefully to their opinions. In any case compromise might not turn out to be a bad thing.

15 WEDNESDAY ☿   *Moon Age Day 4   Moon Sign Libra*

Your intuition is likely to prove extremely good today and with the lunar high pushing you along there is no limit to what you can comfortably achieve. Things need to change in certain areas and you will recognise this instinctively. Don't be at all surprised if you turn out to be flavour of the month in a big way now.

16 THURSDAY ☿   *Moon Age Day 5   Moon Sign Libra*

You should now be feeling very dynamic and active. There are gains to be made in terms of money and Lady Luck is certainly going to be on your side when it matters the most. Travel is high on your agenda and this would be an ideal time for a holiday or some sort of short break that is arranged at more or less the last moment.

17 FRIDAY ☿   *Moon Age Day 6   Moon Sign Scorpio*

It looks as though matters should be falling quite nicely into place around this time of this month. This is especially true in a career sense and with regard to more personal matters. You seem to be fairly organised at present and to have a good idea as to how others are likely to react under any given set of circumstances.

18 SATURDAY ☿   *Moon Age Day 7   Moon Sign Scorpio*

Show a little caution if at all possible. This is a day when it would be sensible not to get on the wrong side of those in authority. You are prepared to stick up for yourself and others in what could be called a reckless manner. Think before you speak and don't take a specific stance you know is certain to annoy someone important.

19 SUNDAY   *Moon Age Day 8   Moon Sign Sagittarius*

Getting ahead in life during today and tomorrow is just as much about charm and personality as it is about really knowing what you are doing. Show the true Libran qualities within you this Sunday. Any chance to get away from the normal routines of the weekend should be firmly grasped with both hands.

20 MONDAY *Moon Age Day 9   Moon Sign Sagittarius*

This is the time of the month when you get the most from groups and from your encounters out in the world. Show what you can do and don't be afraid to be firmly in the spotlight. It might seem as if there is a lot to get done but day by day you are getting towards some of your chosen destinations.

21 TUESDAY *Moon Age Day 10   Moon Sign Sagittarius*

You could benefit now from taking a more direct approach to certain issues. Waiting for things to happen is less successful under present planetary trends than going out there and getting what you want. There are plenty of people around who will think the way you do and most of them would be willing to offer you some support.

22 WEDNESDAY *Moon Age Day 11   Moon Sign Capricorn*

Co-operative endeavours are on the cards, during a month that turns out to be generally excellent for sharing with others. You don't have quite the same incentive to go it alone that might sometimes be the case and you recognise how important it can be to have people alongside you. Libra is a social animal, especially now.

23 THURSDAY *Moon Age Day 12   Moon Sign Capricorn*

You may be on holiday at this time but whether you are or not you can get a great deal from the season and what it offers. Much of your time is likely to be spent out of doors and alongside people who are thinking up ever-better ways to have fun. Family trends are also good and young people especially may give you cause to be proud.

24 FRIDAY *Moon Age Day 13   Moon Sign Aquarius*

A good social trend continues and this could make it somewhat difficult to take the practical and professional side of life quite as seriously as you perhaps should. Never mind, there is plenty of time to worry about such things once the weather turns cold again. For the moment you need to find ever more new ways to enjoy yourself.

25 SATURDAY   *Moon Age Day 14   Moon Sign Aquarius*

There could be a fairly heavy competitive element beginning to appear in your life as a whole. This can apply at work but also even in social or sporting activities. You won't like to lose at anything and you have an insatiable desire to be at the front of any queue. That's fine but just don't allow yourself to become too pushy.

26 SUNDAY   *Moon Age Day 15   Moon Sign Aquarius*

You now gain speed and the best that can be said about the hectic pace of your life today is that it could lead you towards certain realisations about yourself and the way your world is running. A lack-lustre performance is possible if you are at work, but only because you find it hard to concentrate on specifics just at the moment.

27 MONDAY   *Moon Age Day 16   Moon Sign Pisces*

Your best area of operations at the moment is likely to be in one-to-one relationships. The start of a new working week also sees you achieving a deeper relationship with some of the people you work with. If you are between jobs at the moment or have just started a new occupation, this is a time when exciting things can happen.

28 TUESDAY   *Moon Age Day 17   Moon Sign Pisces*

The emphasis is now thrown on to work matters and your ability to re-organise things so that you work more efficiently. At the same time you are slightly torn because the last thing you want at the moment is to be tied to one place or one set of circumstances. Where possible, this is a time for Libra to break out.

29 WEDNESDAY   *Moon Age Day 18   Moon Sign Aries*

Emotional relationships ought to be warm and comfortable at this time, inclining you more towards home and family than your commitments out there in the practical world. If you are busy getting used to something that is slightly different about your life, take it slow and steady. Rushing won't help anything.

30 THURSDAY
Moon Age Day 19   Moon Sign Aries

A little cheek goes a long way and if ever there was a day for taking liberties, this seems to be it. With more energy, plus a greater chance of getting ahead, present trends suggest that you could be well up in the estimation of people who have real influence, which is a real boon. Allow your nature to shine.

31 FRIDAY
Moon Age Day 20   Moon Sign Aries

Be careful not to overlook financial obligations and responsibilities. It is possible that you would rather forget about money for the moment, especially if things are just a little tight, but that isn't really the best way forward. The more you concentrate on issues at this time, the better chance you have to get them sorted out.

September 2018

1 SATURDAY
Moon Age Day 21   Moon Sign Taurus

An optimistic and light-hearted interlude breaks out – and thank goodness for it! The planet Venus is especially useful to you at the moment and it can bring a lot of joy and happiness into your life. You do need a high degree of freedom at the moment and you certainly won't respond well to anyone who tries to hold you back.

2 SUNDAY
Moon Age Day 22   Moon Sign Taurus

Generally speaking you are well able to take care of what is yours around now. Although you are never selfish you will want to protect your investments in a number of ways and you won't be happy with people who seek to interfere in your practical life. Socially speaking you should be riding high at present.

3 MONDAY
Moon Age Day 23   Moon Sign Gemini

Career developments now become possible and even likely. You should be feeling a good deal clearer about your objectives and you won't shy away from the sort of changes that might have seemed extremely unlikely only a very short time ago. Acting on impulse is common for you but more likely now in a social sense.

4 TUESDAY
Moon Age Day 24   Moon Sign Gemini

You are presently best suited to doing things that keep you fully occupied, especially at work. If you have been very dissatisfied with your career in the recent past now could be the best time to look around for something different. You have good luck on your side and a knowing knack of making yourself popular.

5 WEDNESDAY   *Moon Age Day 25   Moon Sign Cancer*

You might feel that you have to fight to get ahead in some ways but the effort should be worthwhile, especially when it comes to finances and personal objectives. Not everyone is going to be on your side at this time but when it matters the most people are likely to come good for you. New adventures now become possible.

6 THURSDAY   *Moon Age Day 26   Moon Sign Cancer*

If you can travel now it should put a smile on your face and give you something exciting to think about. This is important because if there is one thing you can't stand it's a dull life with nothing in store. Actually there is plenty going on but you might have to think hard in order to realise the full potential.

7 FRIDAY   *Moon Age Day 27   Moon Sign Leo*

You are a busy person at the moment and you really do need to get on with your life. This will only be a problem when other people are putting their problems on your shoulders and not helping you out. You can take on a certain amount of responsibility for relatives and friends but there comes a time when people have to manage.

8 SATURDAY   *Moon Age Day 28   Moon Sign Leo*

One of your greatest talents is your ability to tune in to the deepest emotional signals that come from other people. You are always good at this but especially so around now. You may well surprise a few people by knowing exactly what is going in on their heads, maybe even before they realise it themselves.

9 SUNDAY   *Moon Age Day 0   Moon Sign Virgo*

Leisure and entertainment are just the tonic you need right now in order to prevent you from taking yourself or anyone else too seriously. You won't be especially patient at the moment and you could easily fall out with people you see as being unnecessarily stupid. Stand up for someone who is timid.

10 MONDAY
Moon Age Day 1   Moon Sign Virgo

The obligations you feel towards others could prove to be something of a trial for the moment and you may decide to allow them to do whatever they choose instead. Of course this state of affairs won't last and you will still end up running the show. You can't help getting involved, even when you promise yourself you will not do so.

11 TUESDAY
Moon Age Day 2   Moon Sign Libra

You should now do well in pioneering ventures and any tendency to be hesitant or nervy is likely to be out of the window. There is good scope for enlarging your personal horizons and no difficulty whatsoever when it comes to making the best of impressions on others. You can afford to chance your arm on occasions today.

12 WEDNESDAY
Moon Age Day 3   Moon Sign Libra

Good fortune seems to be behind your most important decisions in the middle of this particular week and you won't have any difficulty at all persuading others to follow you anywhere. It should be full steam ahead as far as your career is concerned and when it comes to getting your own way you should be excellent right now.

13 THURSDAY
Moon Age Day 4   Moon Sign Scorpio

People will probably be seeking your advice around now. That's not so surprising because although you can sometimes make some terrible gaffs regarding your own life the advice you give to others is generally very sound. In social matters you will probably be acting on impulse and also maybe planning for a special weekend to come.

14 FRIDAY
Moon Age Day 5   Moon Sign Scorpio

Now is a good time to consolidate, to organise your affairs and to rearrange your living situation in some way. You have what it takes to cut through any amount of red tape and to get on well with all practicalities. On the way you can be of tremendous help to other people, especially those who have been rather confused of late.

15 SATURDAY   *Moon Age Day 6   Moon Sign Scorpio*

Personal matters might have a bearing on your capabilities in the outside world and you really need to keep the two as separate as possible. Something being said to you now will come like a bolt from the blue but it is certainly not going to be in any way adverse. You show a slightly untypical timid tendency for a day or two.

16 SUNDAY   *Moon Age Day 7   Moon Sign Sagittarius*

This may not be the best day of the month for exercising superior judgement. Your mind can be a little clouded by events you can't control and it looks as though you will have a few worries to deal with. These are of no real importance but things tend to stay in your mind and you are now more likely to dwell on them.

17 MONDAY   *Moon Age Day 8   Moon Sign Sagittarius*

Work and your profession generally are likely to occupy you almost fully at the beginning of this week. This is where you are putting in the most effort and where the greatest success can come. You won't be forgetting social or romantic matters but these take second place, for the first part of the week at least.

18 TUESDAY   *Moon Age Day 9   Moon Sign Capricorn*

Intimate matters are positively highlighted and you have a tendency to want to get on with things immediately, even when those closest to you are less keen to do so. You may also be slightly argumentative under certain circumstances and you need to guard against going off at a tangent in practical matters. This is a somewhat confused day.

19 WEDNESDAY   *Moon Age Day 10   Moon Sign Capricorn*

Since you might find it somewhat difficult to make compromises today, you will have to try that much harder to do so. You won't get too far if you insist on getting your own way all the time and you should be aware that others do have your best interests at heart, even if it doesn't always seem that way at first.

20 THURSDAY *Moon Age Day 11   Moon Sign Aquarius*

Now you come to an excellent time for travel. You will be happy to drop everything if a suitable invitation comes along and there is no way you will be tied to mundane routines right now. Your mind is filled with the possibilities that come with far-flung destinations and thoughts of people living very different lives far away.

21 FRIDAY *Moon Age Day 12   Moon Sign Aquarius*

Domestic and family matters are now more fulfilling than they have been and they represent an important part of today's events. At what may be the end of a working week for you, the chances are you will look back at what you have achieved and be satisfied. The trouble at the moment is that there is always something more to do.

22 SATURDAY *Moon Age Day 13   Moon Sign Aquarius*

Your personality now shines brightly and this may be the most sociable and friendly time of the month as far as you are concerned. Love looks good and you can easily find the right words to let someone know how you feel about them. Use your strong will to further your ambitious ends and do what you can to brighten the lives of friends.

23 SUNDAY *Moon Age Day 14   Moon Sign Pisces*

Today an intense emotion can manifest itself in self-analysis or the even greater desire to understand others. It is easy for you to find words to express your love and romance can play a really important part in your life at this time. The attitude of a particular friend might be surprising and you will want to find out why.

24 MONDAY *Moon Age Day 15   Moon Sign Pisces*

Today should be fine and fairly settled. You are likely to be more peaceful inside your mind than has been the case for a while and you can settle to things in a way that has been impossible. The lunar low is just around the corner so it might be sensible to put the finishing touches to certain jobs today. A quieter time is in view.

25 TUESDAY
Moon Age Day 16   Moon Sign Aries

Don't expect miracles from plans and objectives today. The fact is that with the lunar low around you should be happy to hold your own. Temporary setbacks might prove to be unavoidable and you may have to show a great deal of patience when you are up against people who seem determined to throw a spanner in the works.

26 WEDNESDAY
Moon Age Day 17   Moon Sign Aries

Emotions are likely to be close to the surface today and even if these are not yours they can have a bearing on your day. Although you will maintain your sense of humour the same can probably not be said for those around you. Picking up the pieces when someone else is having emotional trouble could be your lot for the moment.

27 THURSDAY
Moon Age Day 18   Moon Sign Aries

Take care today not to push yourself too hard or to fall back into your recent trend of wanting to alter everything just for the sake of it. You can have a really comfortable and happy day but in order to achieve this you must be prepared to leave some things alone and to settle for a steady sort of pace.

28 FRIDAY
Moon Age Day 19   Moon Sign Taurus

It's a fact that you cannot please all of the people all of the time, a saying that is likely to make real sense to you today. There are times when it is pointless trying and, in the end, all you can do is your best. Some people might disbelieve even that but that's the way life is. Keep smiling today.

29 SATURDAY
Moon Age Day 20   Moon Sign Taurus

You need to be careful because extreme restlessness is possible today. This is because you have been working hard for so long and might now find yourself with time on your hands. That's great because it means you can find some way to unwind. Grab a friend and do something that isn't important but is enjoyable all the same.

133

30 SUNDAY
Moon Age Day 21   Moon Sign Gemini

It looks as though relationships of almost any sort can be emotionally uplifting but where love and romance are concerned, the world should be your oyster right now. Your confidence is stronger in personal rather than professional situations. You could be on the receiving end of a very special favour.

October

2018

1 MONDAY
Moon Age Day 22   Moon Sign Gemini

Today could be a time of deep insight and you may have the feeling that life is laid out for you in a much clearer way than is sometimes the case. You can help loved ones in practical ways and this ability also extends to work, where colleagues will be more than pleased to accept your advice and your willingness to pitch in.

2 TUESDAY
Moon Age Day 23   Moon Sign Cancer

You need to seek the wide blue yonder and a late holiday won't be out of the question for some Librans around this time. Even if you can't get away for a lengthy break perhaps you could take a few hours out to do whatever takes your fancy. What will rankle at the moment is having to do what others tell you.

3 WEDNESDAY
Moon Age Day 24   Moon Sign Cancer

It's great to travel, especially if you are a Libran. Take off on a little adventure if you get the chance. You certainly won't do yourself any good at all by sticking around at home all the time and present planetary trends virtually demand a change of scenery. Intellectual pastimes are the most rewarding ones in which to indulge.

4 THURSDAY
Moon Age Day 25   Moon Sign Leo

As usual you will be perpetually on the go and also as normal you will positively hate any sort of routine you see as outmoded and boring. Make use of your natural sense of what's right and dress to impress when you get the chance. This can be especially important in professional settings or for a social function.

5 FRIDAY
Moon Age Day 26   Moon Sign Leo

You work best when you are free to make your own decisions today – a trend that has been obvious for quite some time. It really is too much to expect you to toe any line you don't care for and you could be quite cross if you discover that you have no choice in the matter. Try to stay cool, calm and collected as much as you can today.

6 SATURDAY
Moon Age Day 27   Moon Sign Virgo

Today you are very candid and will brush aside any tendency on the part of others to take over your life. It looks as though this is a recurring theme but things will change significantly in only a few days. Continue to do all you can to welcome newcomers into your social circle because new friends can be made.

7 SUNDAY
Moon Age Day 28   Moon Sign Virgo

Look out for important news, some of which is likely to come from rather surprising directions. There are pointers to your future if you watch what is happening in your immediate vicinity and no job is beneath your dignity today if you think it will impress someone or achieve a desired objective. Libra is fully positive.

8 MONDAY
Moon Age Day 29   Moon Sign Virgo

In personal relationships you can now be slightly provocative, though you are also quite fascinating and people will be happy to have you around. Lively discussions are likely all day long and with a number of different types of people. Avoid constant attention to detail at the moment because it will wear you out.

9 TUESDAY
Moon Age Day 0   Moon Sign Libra

Progress should be easy to achieve today. The lunar high is likely to make you feel brighter, freer and more inclined to take chances. Any sluggish tendencies of the last couple of weeks will disappear and you should be on top form, especially in terms of your social and love life. Stand by for some outrageous possibilities.

10 WEDNESDAY   *Moon Age Day 1   Moon Sign Libra*

The green light is now definitely on and there isn't much that will hold you back once you decide the time is right for action. A little positive thinking goes a very long way under present trends and you have what it takes to impress the most important people in your life. Love shines strongly in your direction, and you reflect it wonderfully.

11 THURSDAY   *Moon Age Day 2   Moon Sign Scorpio*

You will probably have more sympathy for the underdog today and will do all you can to help people who are having problems of one sort or another. You are clearly very concerned for everyone around you and though this is to be praised you might just be doing rather more than you reasonably should in at least one case later today.

12 FRIDAY   *Moon Age Day 3   Moon Sign Scorpio*

Social relationships may be a cause of some frustration right now and you need to be right on form when it comes to the way you speak to people. This isn't at all difficult for Libra as you can be charm itself when you need to be. This is especially important when you are dealing with superiors or people with great influence.

13 SATURDAY   *Moon Age Day 4   Moon Sign Sagittarius*

There is now a more hurried feel to your everyday life and everything seems as though it is happening at the same time. There won't be time right now to get hung up on details and you will be dealing with those matters that can be sorted out and finished in little or no time. Anything complicated should be left for another day.

14 SUNDAY   *Moon Age Day 5   Moon Sign Sagittarius*

Disagreements can arise at home or in almost any situation where you have to follow the lead of people you either don't trust or don't respect. A greater degree of co-operation is called for but don't expect it to be easy now to come to terms with certain people. Part of the trouble is that you are so original yourself.

15 MONDAY   *Moon Age Day 6   Moon Sign Capricorn*

Professionally speaking you could be somewhat overstretched now by someone in authority. At home it is likely that your ability to get on well with others is not quite as obvious today. It could be that you are rebelling against people who are making demands on you that you are not willing to accommodate.

16 TUESDAY   *Moon Age Day 7   Moon Sign Capricorn*

As a rule you hate to be stuck in any sort of routine but this is less likely to be the case under present trends. On the contrary you will take comfort from doing things in the same old way – a fact that might come as a surprise to some of your friends. Don't worry though because even by tomorrow you will be back to normal.

17 WEDNESDAY   *Moon Age Day 8   Moon Sign Capricorn*

A phase of strong personal magnetism is at hand and today is a period during which it ought to be easier to influence other people than it has been of late. Be determined and you can't go far wrong. At this stage of the week you might be slightly concerned about money, though probably not for very long.

18 THURSDAY   *Moon Age Day 9   Moon Sign Aquarius*

There seems to be no way of getting ahead today that doesn't mean doing what someone else wants you to do. This definitely goes against the grain but will prove to be necessary. To refuse to take part would be to cut off your nose to spite your face. Of course you can be stubborn but that won't do you any good at all.

19 FRIDAY   *Moon Age Day 10   Moon Sign Aquarius*

Now you appear to be very career-oriented and will want to put as much energy as possible into getting ahead professionally. You excel at managing or supervising others, even if you have not been earmarked to do so. It's just that at present you are a natural leader and you can't avoid taking control.

20 SATURDAY
Moon Age Day 11   Moon Sign Pisces

If you are clever, you can be extremely persuasive today and can get more or less everything you want without having to put in too much in the way of hard, physical work. Socially speaking you seem to be on top form and have what it takes to show yourself in a very favourable light when it matters the most.

21 SUNDAY
Moon Age Day 12   Moon Sign Pisces

It is towards the practical world that you can now look for some genuine support. Some of your plans need slightly more than thought and you may have to put in some real effort to get over a particular hurdle. On the way you can find moments of real fun, most likely in the company of people you think of as being your best friends.

22 MONDAY
Moon Age Day 13   Moon Sign Pisces

Your role in group activities seems to be highlighted now. You will be feeling distinctly optimistic, willing to fall in line with any reasonable request and you are flexible enough to change your direction at a moment's notice. Give yourself a pat on the back for a success that is a direct result of your hard work.

23 TUESDAY
Moon Age Day 14   Moon Sign Aries

The lunar low this month gives you an ideal opportunity to overcome difficulties and achieve your objectives. It's true that there are circumstances that might seem at first to hold you back but you also have a strong determination and a sense of purpose. One thing at once is the best adage; so don't crowd your schedule too much.

24 WEDNESDAY
Moon Age Day 15   Moon Sign Aries

You could feel a little cut off from life in some ways but there is a great deal of personal choice about this and you will probably feel quite happy to spend at least some time on your own. It might be difficult to do when you are surrounded by noise and activity, but think things through. Libra is very pensive today.

25 THURSDAY   *Moon Age Day 16   Moon Sign Taurus*

A little discontent could arise in personal attachments, even though this is more or less forced upon you by circumstances. For this reason alone you are less likely to be spending a great deal of time thinking about romance and will be inclined to dwell more in the practical world. You are likely to be thinking a lot about money.

26 FRIDAY   *Moon Age Day 17   Moon Sign Taurus*

This should be a fantastic period for putting new plans into action. With everything to play for and a feeling of great confidence, you can now put the finishing touch to something that has been waiting for quite a while. What is most noticeable about today is the way you are able to manipulate situations to suit your own needs.

27 SATURDAY   *Moon Age Day 18   Moon Sign Gemini*

Look to friends for both support and fulfilment. Whether you realise it or not you are coming to the end of one particular phase in your life and new things need to be allowed in. There's no problem about this as far as you are concerned and you should be quite willing to wear almost any sort of clothes on your journey to better times.

28 SUNDAY   *Moon Age Day 19   Moon Sign Gemini*

Opportunities that present themselves today probably won't come again for quite a while so focus fully on life. The need to pay attention means you should concentrate on one thing at a time – never an easy task for Libra. You should now be more inclined to analyse your past efforts with a desire to improve.

29 MONDAY   *Moon Age Day 20   Moon Sign Cancer*

Your vitality, natural sense of fun and your charm are likely to make you popular with most people. The odd person who doesn't care for you all that much can now be ignored because you are too busy to acknowledge them. This would be a great time to join new groups of clubs but do make sure you are not just doing so on a whim.

30 TUESDAY   *Moon Age Day 21   Moon Sign Cancer*

What you are looking at now is great potential for personal growth. Lessons can be learned from situations that are winding down now, or which have come to a logical pause. When you apply yourself to them again or start something new, you will have gained a great deal in terms of experience and contentment.

31 WEDNESDAY   *Moon Age Day 22   Moon Sign Cancer*

It looks as though you are going to be very plain spoken in your dealings with others, especially at work. You won't take no for an answer on those occasions when you are certain of your ground and you seem to be at your most dynamic professionally. At home you will be more relaxed but will still have very definite opinions.

November 2018

1 THURSDAY
Moon Age Day 23   Moon Sign Leo

Making certain dreams into realities now becomes possible, though a little extra effort will be necessary to make the procedure work well. Whether or not you will still want what you desired once it becomes possible, remains to be seen. It is very important to be specific about your requirements in the days and weeks ahead.

2 FRIDAY
Moon Age Day 24   Moon Sign Leo

Your career should prove to be the most important, and possibly also the most interesting, sphere of your life today. Not that you are also lacking when it comes to having a good time. Your ability to mix business with pleasure has probably never been so well developed and it is possible to make good friends from colleagues.

3 SATURDAY
Moon Age Day 25   Moon Sign Virgo

It looks as though your popularity is going to be a major issue. It is possible that you are trying too hard, which really isn't necessary. Just relax and be yourself. When it comes to romance you are likely to be right in the swing of things and showing just how sexy you are capable of being. Look after the pennies for the moment.

4 SUNDAY
Moon Age Day 26   Moon Sign Virgo

Involve yourself as much as possible in group activities and make sure you get together with people who have similar views to your own. Not that there will be any trouble in adapting to different types, but your greatest successes at the moment are likely to come when there is a strong meeting of minds.

5 MONDAY
Moon Age Day 27   Moon Sign Libra

This is the best day of the month to break loose and to do whatever takes your fancy. If your time is your own early this week you will want to spend it having fun in good company. Your amazing capacity for successfully mixing business with pleasure should do you a great deal of good at the same time.

6 TUESDAY
Moon Age Day 28   Moon Sign Libra

A high degree of good fortune is likely to attend your life right now and you can make gains by simply being in the right place and by following your intuition. Money matters should take a turn for the better, even if it is only a case of sorting things out in your own mind. Most important of all today is the opportunity to enjoy yourself.

7 WEDNESDAY
Moon Age Day 0   Moon Sign Scorpio

Your career ambitions should be running well, though probably below the surface just for the moment. You sense that superiors are studying you carefully and you will need to give of your best, working quietly but confidently between now and the weekend. Once you are away from work there could be some surprises in store.

8 THURSDAY
Moon Age Day 1   Moon Sign Scorpio

As far as relationships are concerned at this time love matches can be a way to expand your personal horizons and to learn more about life in general. Not that you are restricting yourself in terms of the people you mix with. On the contrary you are very approachable and as interesting to be with as Libra nearly always turns out to be.

9 FRIDAY
Moon Age Day 2   Moon Sign Sagittarius

Life can be a constant learning process and this is certainly the case for the typical Libran. Don't assume today that you know everything about any topic. There are always going to be people who can tell you something new and the more you pay attention the greater will be your appreciation of life's nuances.

10 SATURDAY   *Moon Age Day 3   Moon Sign Sagittarius*

Family matters are accentuated today. You can benefit from the comforts of home and also from activities that are taking place there. There are strong emotional ties at work in your thinking and you will not make many decisions today without seeking the advice of your partner or family members who always offer sound counsel.

11 SUNDAY   *Moon Age Day 4   Moon Sign Sagittarius*

Expect career boosts to be coming along at any time now, though of course probably not on a Sunday. Nevertheless you can do yourself some professional good by thinking through your strategy for next week. You may also be very drawn towards sport under present trends and will be happy to test yourself in some way.

12 MONDAY   *Moon Age Day 5   Moon Sign Capricorn*

You are now looking towards higher purposes and such is the complicated working of your mind that at least some other people won't understand you at all. Try to get together with those individuals who are as unique and far-sighted as you are. Your confidence to do the right thing in relationships is clearly growing now.

13 TUESDAY   *Moon Age Day 6   Moon Sign Capricorn*

It's time to discover the new or the unusual that exists all around you. How exciting life can be and how keen you are to know everything about it. You thrive best when you are educating yourself about the world and that is certainly something you tend to do at this time. New starts at work may be beneficial in the longer-term.

14 WEDNESDAY   *Moon Age Day 7   Moon Sign Aquarius*

Contentious matters are likely to arise and you may find it difficult to get away from issues you would rather ignore altogether. In a personal sense you seem to be making a good impression on someone you find attractive and you might also discover you have an admirer you didn't suspect. Whether that pleases you remains to be seen.

15 THURSDAY   *Moon Age Day 8   Moon Sign Aquarius*

Independence and anything unusual are both issues for today. Routine is not a word you want to hear for the moment and you will value anyone who is as 'off the wall' as you are at times. Keep up the good work when it comes to projecting your image on to a bigger and bigger audience and do all you can to be heard.

16 FRIDAY   *Moon Age Day 9   Moon Sign Aquarius*

It's just possible that a social contact on which you are inclined to rely may well be missing for now and perhaps the foreseeable future. This might mean having to stand on your own feet. The lessons learned are positive for you because necessity is the mother of invention. You learn some important facts about yourself.

17 SATURDAY   ☿   *Moon Age Day 10   Moon Sign Pisces*

This could be one of your most pleasurable days as far as social trends go and it seems you are more than willing to drop some of the responsibilities of life in order to have a good time. This is achieved in the company of people you like to be close to. Some of the compliments that come your way today are disguised but well meant.

18 SUNDAY   ☿   *Moon Age Day 11   Moon Sign Pisces*

This can be a very positive sort of Sunday but you need to be as free from restrictions as you can manage. There may be people around who seem to hold you back and prevent you from making the progress you would wish. In the 'seesaw' environment you inhabit just at present, it is important to keep trying to break away.

19 MONDAY   ☿   *Moon Age Day 12   Moon Sign Aries*

If you are tired today you can at least partly blame the lunar low. This might not be the most dynamic period of the year but it can be warm and comfortable, with much to recommend it in a personal sense. Recognise that people are on your side and the best sort of reassurance is not likely to be far away.

20 TUESDAY ☿ *Moon Age Day 13 Moon Sign Aries*

This is likely to be another day that lacks some of the sparkle you are always seeking but you can still enjoy yourself if you don't have too many expectations. Rules and regulations could easily bother you and although you feel most secure at home you could even feel somewhat tied down there. A few small excursions might help.

21 WEDNESDAY ☿ *Moon Age Day 14 Moon Sign Taurus*

You may have conflicts today with people you're close to. Try to avoid getting embroiled in disputes that can't really help and will only actually hinder your progress. Differences of opinion, though inevitable, can be sorted out rationally. In terms of cash you could discover you are slightly better off than you thought.

22 THURSDAY ☿ *Moon Age Day 15 Moon Sign Taurus*

Whilst it seems plain that your nearest and dearest have your best interests at heart, you could still be having a little trouble with the way they go about trying to help you. Librans are independently minded at this stage and there is little of nothing you can do to redress this balance. Everything should settle down by tomorrow.

23 FRIDAY ☿ *Moon Age Day 16 Moon Sign Taurus*

Now you should find far more beneficial social trends developing, together with a better reaction on your part to the fact that your partner is so keen to get involved in aspects of your life they might have ignored before. Think seriously about an offer that has come in regarding your work and you might just opt for change.

24 SATURDAY ☿ *Moon Age Day 17 Moon Sign Gemini*

Your focus at this time tends to be mainly towards career or practical jobs if you do not work. At home you will also find yourself pretty well committed to getting things done and you tend to be very efficient in the way you manage your time. Look out for the odd sprain or strain – probably brought about by trying too hard physically.

25 SUNDAY   ☿   *Moon Age Day 18   Moon Sign Gemini*

Personal relationships could be subject to a few misunderstandings so work hard to resolve these early in the day if they do arise. Compromises at this time can lead to a smoother life and you will feel much better about everything if you get on well with those around you. Look out for an unexpected gain.

26 MONDAY   ☿   *Moon Age Day 19   Moon Sign Cancer*

This is one of those days on which you can never be sure what you can learn if you keep your eyes and ears open. Even the most casual of conversations can lead you to understanding something that was a total mystery to you before and you have what it takes to make failure into glorious victory. Things are starting to look good.

27 TUESDAY   ☿   *Moon Age Day 20   Moon Sign Cancer*

You will now get more than a little help from your friends and there are plenty of positive highlights surrounding social occasions. Of course there is also time for work but you are even turning this into a joy and mixing it with friendship and compromise. The world is now starting to see the very best of what Libra can be.

28 WEDNESDAY ☿   *Moon Age Day 21   Moon Sign Leo*

You may be feeling a little stale about certain aspects of your life and a Libran desire to change things comes upon you once again. That's fine but don't throw out the baby with the bathwater. Some things are tried and tested and need to stay as they are in order to offer you greater security. It's just a case of working out what to do.

29 THURSDAY   ☿   *Moon Age Day 22   Moon Sign Leo*

Though much is moving forward in your life around now, there could be a feeling that you have forgotten something important. Put aside a little time to try and work out what it might be but don't go mad because you could just as easily be suffering from a slight bout of insecurity. In the main, life should now be going your way.

30 FRIDAY ☿ *Moon Age Day 23   Moon Sign Virgo*

You would prefer nothing to hold you back at present, though life rarely works that way and, in any case, some kickback sharpens your intellect and makes you think more deeply. Having to struggle to get your point across is useful, though you could stand a chance of falling into a trap of your own making if you are not careful.

December

2018

1 SATURDAY ☿ *Moon Age Day 24 Moon Sign Virgo*

Be a little careful right now because your emotional suggestibility is at its highest. Right now you tend to believe exactly what you want to believe and that can be something of a mistake. People are generally kind, but there could be the odd selfish individual and that is the one you need to watch out for.

2 SUNDAY ☿ *Moon Age Day 25 Moon Sign Libra*

A result of the enthusiasm you invest in all matters, a little good fortune should now be coming your way. Although this probably won't be anything major it will be important to you and can pave the way to greater successes later on. Give some time to your partner and find ways to have fun that you have not tried before.

3 MONDAY ☿ *Moon Age Day 26 Moon Sign Libra*

Now you should be overflowing with ideas and more willing than ever to test your luck. There should be plenty going on around you in a social sense and you will want to do all you can to make the most of new situations and positive meetings. Give yourself time later in the day to show your concern for family members.

4 TUESDAY ☿ *Moon Age Day 27 Moon Sign Scorpio*

Your chief ability at work now is likely to be your ability to establish contact with other people on an intense level. Communication is now the key to success. There isn't anything particularly unusual about this fact as far as you are concerned but it is the depth of the ties you establish that are proving to be so important at this time.

5 WEDNESDAY ☿ *Moon Age Day 28 Moon Sign Scorpio*

In a professional sense you are best suited to a situation in which you have contact with any number of other people. In this way you can use many of your ideas and you actively need the response that these bring. It is quite likely that some unexpected assistance will come along at some time during today.

6 THURSDAY ☿ *Moon Age Day 29 Moon Sign Scorpio*

A slightly slower and more studied approach to plans and objectives seems to be in order around this time. Keep to one or two simple priorities and try not to crowd your schedule more than is absolutely necessary. In addition to being busy in a practical sense it may only now have occurred to you now that Christmas is getting closer

7 FRIDAY *Moon Age Day 0 Moon Sign Sagittarius*

Your own drives and feelings might be slightly at odds with those of the people you are mixing with most freely. This means there is the possibility of a disagreement you could quite easily do without at this time. It would be better under most circumstances today to withdraw from any issue that looks as though it might get out of control.

8 SATURDAY *Moon Age Day 1 Moon Sign Sagittarius*

You are clearly eager to make a good impression and to get on well with just about everyone. That's fine but it may not be possible under all circumstances. Some people seem determined to be awkward and you may have to disagree with them. However, this doesn't mean your popularity is going to disappear overnight, or at all.

9 SUNDAY *Moon Age Day 2 Moon Sign Capricorn*

Watch out because there might be some unrealistic fantasies to deal with today, mainly coming from the direction of your friends or perhaps family members. On the plus side the romantic possibilities look especially intriguing and potentially rewarding now.

10 MONDAY   *Moon Age Day 3   Moon Sign Capricorn*

It looks as though you will be quite attached to your work at this time and you won't take kindly to anyone trying to pull the professional rug from under you. Your ideas now tend to be creative and progress and decisions you make at this time ought to show very good judgement. Treat the secrets of your friends with great respect.

11 TUESDAY   *Moon Age Day 4   Moon Sign Aquarius*

True to your fun loving Libran nature you function best at the moment when you are involved in a team or some sort of social group. Whether you are working or simply finding ways to have fun this should turn out to be an eventful and generally rewarding day.

12 WEDNESDAY   *Moon Age Day 5   Moon Sign Aquarius*

Right now you are very impressionable and will be easily influenced by others. There's nothing wrong with this just as long as you are aware that not everyone is as honest or decent as you are. There could be times today when you will be happy to withdraw.

13 THURSDAY   *Moon Age Day 6   Moon Sign Aquarius*

In a social sense it looks as though trends continue to be very favourable. Groups of people provide the greatest stimulus at the moment and your general motto seems to be 'the more the merrier'. Parties will be forthcoming and gatherings with the sort of people who give you good ideas. Mixing and mingling is now second nature.

14 FRIDAY   *Moon Age Day 7   Moon Sign Pisces*

What happens today in personal relationships might be far from inspiring – at least at first. However, you should not underestimate your own ability to bring people round to your point of view. With a little determination and plenty of Libran know-how you can work wonders. Keep an eye on money right now.

15 SATURDAY   *Moon Age Day 8   Moon Sign Pisces*

The accent today seems to be on the domestic scene and you will have plenty of time to concentrate on making your nearest and dearest happy. All the same, you don't want life to become dull and you might find ways to integrate family members into your busy social scene. Librans who are presently studying should be doing fine.

16 SUNDAY   *Moon Age Day 9   Moon Sign Pisces*

Today the major focus needs to be on having fun. Even when you are doing the most mundane of jobs you can find ways to make them seem more exciting and you can also inspire others to do things for you. The general path of life at the moment is towards greater success, even if there are a few diversions on the way.

17 MONDAY   *Moon Age Day 10   Moon Sign Aries*

Some of your plans for today might have to be altered at the last minute but the way to deal with the odd difficult situation is to react by instinct – something you are very good at doing. You won't feel the need to travel now and will probably enjoy a stay-at-home sort of Monday if that proves to be possible.

18 TUESDAY   *Moon Age Day 11   Moon Sign Aries*

Perhaps you will be slightly quieter for the moment and if this is the case you can thank the presence of the Moon in your opposite zodiac sign. This is a state of affairs that you deal with every month and it is intended to be a time to plan for more progressive times. Take time out to contact a distant friend.

19 WEDNESDAY   *Moon Age Day 12   Moon Sign Taurus*

Your social skills are now increased and in the roller coaster ride that is life at the moment you are now on your way to the top again. Your ability to make a good impression on people you see as being important has rarely been better than it is at present. Use today to do some of those important jobs at home.

20 THURSDAY   *Moon Age Day 13   Moon Sign Taurus*

Some slight setbacks at the start of today should not be allowed to stop you from moving forward in a generally positive way. Try not to restrict yourself to your own four walls around now but get out and meet people whenever and wherever possible. A few new tricks on your part make for a fun time today.

21 FRIDAY   *Moon Age Day 14   Moon Sign Gemini*

New meetings with others can inspire you to come up with good ideas and you are certainly not likely to slow down the practical and positive side of life just to accommodate the festive season. On the contrary, you might even shelve one or two aspects of Christmas planning in order to pursue something you see as important.

22 SATURDAY   *Moon Age Day 15   Moon Sign Gemini*

This is a time to realise how good your love life can be and a period when it is possible to take a short holiday from the responsibilities that might have been pressing in on you for a while. Socially speaking the trends are excellent and it looks as though the Christmas bug has bitten you at last, even though you held out well.

23 SUNDAY   *Moon Age Day 16   Moon Sign Cancer*

Although this is the start of the festive season and therefore a generally optimistic period as far as you are concerned, there is a slight risk that you will lose your sense of proportion in some situations. Try not to worry and certainly don't dwell upon what might go wrong. In the main you should find this to be a successful day.

24 MONDAY   *Moon Age Day 17   Moon Sign Cancer*

Christmas Eve trends favour a quick and accurate assessment of life's possibilities, plus an insatiable desire to see and do as much as you can. No matter what the weather is doing you will probably want to get out of doors and enjoy the fresh air and you will be quite sure of all your views and opinions at this time.

25 TUESDAY   *Moon Age Day 18   Moon Sign Leo*

Christmas Day finds you optimistic, keen to get out and about and simply bursting to show an unsuspecting world what you are capable of doing. Planetary assistance comes at a most opportune time and it encourages you to leave your own domain and go visiting. Challenges are taken on board willingly and dealt with excellently.

26 WEDNESDAY   *Moon Age Day 19   Moon Sign Leo*

This turns out to be an extremely good time for problem solving. Perhaps take a day out from most of the celebrations, and put your mind to the test. This is always a good exercise for you, though you should not make more out of your findings than is really present. Confidence and optimism remain high.

27 THURSDAY   *Moon Age Day 20   Moon Sign Virgo*

It is quite likely that the period between now and the New Year will be one of movement and merriment. You will be settling to what is expected of you during the holiday break and making the most of the social trends that are looking so good. You may even make the odd financial gain today.

28 FRIDAY   *Moon Age Day 21   Moon Sign Virgo*

This is going to be a great time for social gatherings, at home or at work. Your mind turns away from the practical and towards having fun. What really sets today apart is your popularity and how much you can influence the lives of some people who may not have been going through a good time of late.

29 SATURDAY   *Moon Age Day 22   Moon Sign Libra*

Certain situations are apt to disappear from your life at this time, though most of them are going to be things you are quite happy – even overjoyed – to leave behind. You are on a generally upward trend and today brings you closer to your heart's desire in ways that have little or nothing to do with the festivities.

30 SUNDAY   *Moon Age Day 23   Moon Sign Libra*

Unhealthy habits can be easy to shake off, even though this is generally a part of the year during which excess rules. You are feeling fitter and healthier than has been the case and that makes you want to chase the ideals of perfection that are always in your mind. A reflection of this is just how much others think about you now.

31 MONDAY   *Moon Age Day 24   Moon Sign Libra*

Only you can decide how today is going to go, which infers some responsibility. This doesn't trouble you in the slightest because you should be feeling fitter and more confident than ever. This New Year's Eve, consider the things you need to leave behind, even if many of them are trivial. Have some fun tonight.

RISING SIGNS FOR LIBRA

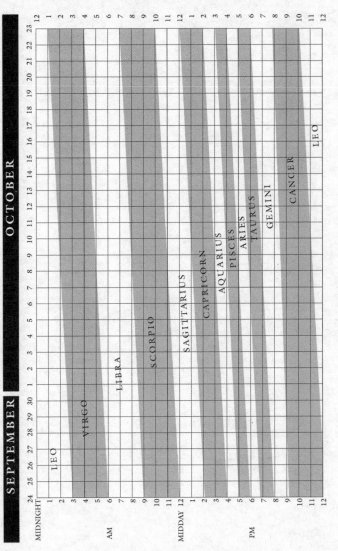

157

THE ZODIAC, PLANETS AND CORRESPONDENCES

The Earth revolves around the Sun once every calendar year, so when viewed from Earth the Sun appears in a different part of the sky as the year progresses. In astrology, these parts of the sky are divided into the signs of the zodiac and this means that the signs are organised in a circle. The circle begins with Aries and ends with Pisces.

Taking the zodiac sign as a starting point, astrologers then work with all the positions of planets, stars and many other factors to calculate horoscopes and birth charts and tell us what the stars have in store for us.

The table below shows the planets and Elements for each of the signs of the zodiac. Each sign belongs to one of the four Elements: Fire, Air, Earth or Water. Fire signs are creative and enthusiastic; Air signs are mentally active and thoughtful; Earth signs are constructive and practical; Water signs are emotional and have strong feelings.

It also shows the metals and gemstones associated with, or corresponding with, each sign. The correspondence is made when a metal or stone possesses properties that are held in common with a particular sign of the zodiac.

Finally, the table shows the opposite of each star sign – this is the opposite sign in the astrological circle.

Placed	Sign	Symbol	Element	Planet	Metal	Stone	Opposite
1	Aries	Ram	Fire	Mars	Iron	Bloodstone	Libra
2	Taurus	Bull	Earth	Venus	Copper	Sapphire	Scorpio
3	Gemini	Twins	Air	Mercury	Mercury	Tiger's Eye	Sagittarius
4	Cancer	Crab	Water	Moon	Silver	Pearl	Capricorn
5	Leo	Lion	Fire	Sun	Gold	Ruby	Aquarius
6	Virgo	Maiden	Earth	Mercury	Mercury	Sardonyx	Pisces
7	Libra	Scales	Air	Venus	Copper	Sapphire	Aries
8	Scorpio	Scorpion	Water	Pluto	Plutonium	Jasper	Taurus
9	Sagittarius	Archer	Fire	Jupiter	Tin	Topaz	Gemini
10	Capricorn	Goat	Earth	Saturn	Lead	Black Onyx	Cancer
11	Aquarius	Waterbearer	Air	Uranus	Uranium	Amethyst	Leo
12	Pisces	Fishes	Water	Neptune	Tin	Moonstone	Virgo